Contents

To Jennifer, Emma and Christopher - my inspiration — J.H.

Been driving 500 miles, got 500 to go, yeah … The ride of my life began on April 19 with the Love It Live Legends Playoff Tour in full bloom, speaking to my basketball heroes on a nightly basis — Abdul-Jabbar, Havlicek, Iceman, Malone, Monroe, Russell, Walton — amazed and inspired with the wealth of knowledge imparted from the men who have contributed immeasurably to the NBA's global appeal … *400 miles*… The ride soon picked up speed … *Well I'm a little hot wired, but I'm feeling alright* … The Spurs' championship drive reflected the very best in teamwork, commitment and execution and the completion of this official NBA Finals Retrospective wasn't any different … *These are better days, baby* … The Admiral, Charlie Rosenzweig pointing the way, setting the highest of standards … *We stood side by side each one fightin' for the other* … Joe Amati and Scott Yurdin of NBA Photos expertly providing the photo direction and painstaking selection, coming through, time and time and time again … *We said until we died we'd always be blood brothers* … Michael Levine, the visionary groom, flawlessly and masterfully overseeing the multitude of details regarding all aspects of this project … *400 miles* … Margaret Williams, applying the meticulous attention to detail, who along with the stellar championship lineup of Mario Argote, David Mintz and Chris Countee, made yours truly look good … *300 miles* … David Bonilla, John Kristofick, Bennett Renda, the men behind the scenes who pulled it all together … At NVU Productions, Jim Forni, Tom O'Grady, Melinda Fry – thank you! … *200 miles* … Steve Polacek (Stevie Franchise), the creative mastermind who spent countless hours in delivering this beautifully designed book, making the pages come to life like never before – wow! … *Is everyone in? The ceremony is about to begin* …Carmin Romanelli, for once again nurturing the creative process … *100 miles* … Andrew Bernstein, Nat Butler and Jesse Garrabrant and the rest of the NBAE crew — the world's greatest photographers — who capture the magic on a nightly basis … *I'm just around the corner till the light of day, yeah* — John Hareas, July 2003

Special Thanks [A T N B A E N T E R T A I N M E N T P H O T O S] Carmin Romanelli, Joe Amati, David Bonilla, Scott Yurdin, Jesse Garrabrant, Pam Healy, Michael Klein, Brian Choi, John Kristofick, Bennett Renda, Ned Dishman and Thomas Oliver [A T N B A E N T E R T A I N M E N T] Adam Silver, Gregg Winik, Heidi Ueberroth, Charles Rosenzweig, Paul Hirschheimer, Marc Hirschheimer, Michael Levine, Mario Argote, David Mintz, Margaret Williams, Chris Countee, Tony Stewart, Rob Sario [A T T H E N B A] David Stern, Russ Granik, Tim Andree, Brian McIntyre, Terry Lyons [A T N V U P R O D U C T I O N S] Jim Forni, Tom O'Grady, Steve Polacek, Melinda Fry, Sue Young [A T P R O F E S S I O N A L G R A P H I C S] David Goley, Jane Messenger and their entire staff [A T I N L A N D P R E S S] Jim Lacy, Marsha Drake and their entire staff [A T T H E S P U R S] Peter Holt, Gregg Popovich, Russ Bookbinder, Lawrence Payne, Bruce Guthrie, Tom James, Becky Salini, Moe Guerrero and the entire Spurs organization

Photography Credits FRONT COVER BY JESSE D. GARRABRANT BACK COVER BY NATHANIEL S. BUTLER, ANDREW D. BERNSTEIN, JED JACOBSOHN, EZRA SHAW ANDREW.D.BERNSTEIN 5, 9, 10, 11, 12, 13, 15, 16, 17, 22, 25, 26, 32, 33, 38, 39, 41, 45, 47, 48, 49, 50, 51, 52, 53, 54, 55, 59, 60, 61, 64, 70, 77, 78, 80, 81, 82, 83, 84, 88, 90, 91, 93, 95, 96, 98, 101, 103, 105, 106, 109, 110, 111 NATHANIEL S.BUTLER 1, 3, 5, 29, 35, 44, 58, 60, 61, 62, 63, 64, 65, 67, 68, 69, 71, 72, 73, 75, 77, 79, 84, 85, 87, 89, 91, 93, 95, 97, 99, 102, 104, 105, 109, 110, 111, 112 JESSE D. GARRABRANT 33, 35, 85, 103, 105, 108 LOU CAPOZZOLA 5, 77, 81, 87, 89, 94 FERNANDO MEDINA 17, 35 GLENN JAMES- 55, 112 RON HOSKINS 17, 19 ROCKY WIDNER 19, 35, 39, 45, 76 PETER READ MILLER 21, BILL BAPTIST 17, 18 D. CLARKE EVANS 5, 13, 31, 35, 37, 39, 43 SAM FORENCICH 35, 36 CATHERINE STEENKESTE 9, 11, 87 BARRY GOSSAGE 7, 23, 49 NOREN TROTMAN 24 ANDY HAYT 25, 27 GARRETT W. ELLWOOD 42, 84 CHIRS COVATTA 43, 61 JENNIFER POTTHEISER 56, 57, 84, 85 M. DAVID LEEDS 84, 85 NOAH GRAHAM 5, 40, 107 RON KOCH 5

Relive the excitement of the 2003 NBA Finals with the Official Championship Home Video and DVD, featuring exclusive behind-the-scenes footage and interviews. Journey into basketball history with the San Antonio Spurs.

TO ORDER LOG ON TO THE NBA STORE AT NBA.COM

Designed by NVU Editions.
Distributed by NVU Editions.

First published in the United States of America in 2003 by NVU Editions, 363 West Erie 4W, Chicago, IL 60610. nvuproductions.com

Photography by NBA Entertainment Photos

Library of Congress Cataloging-in-Publication Data is available from the Publisher

ISBN 0-9724575-8-5

Printed and bound in the Unites States of America.

9 8 7 6 5 3 2
First Edition

THE LEGEND CONTINUES

BY JOHN HAREAS

PHOTOGRAPHY BY NBA ENTERTAINMENT PHOTOS

A JOURNEY OF COMMITMENT, SACRIFICE AND VICTORY

WHAT A WONDERFUL SEASON! IT IS QUITE RARE AND CERTAINLY A GREAT DEAL OF FUN TO WATCH A TEAM DEVELOP AND PERFORM IN SUCH A SYNCHRONIZED AND SELFLESS MANNER — AN OLD SCHOOL TEAM IF YOU WILL.

From the beginning of training camp our coaches (probably the players too) knew there were many unanswered questions about this group concerning the individual abilities in the cases of Emanuel Ginobili, Stephen Jackson, Tony Parker and the acceptance of roles by everyone, especially veterans like Steve Kerr, Steve Smith, Danny Ferry and Kevin Willis.

Our first step was to establish a culture and environment in which to work and put into place the standards we would live by on a day to day basis. I have often heard and read that the will to win must be eclipsed by the will to prepare to win. To the coaches this meant skipping no steps and taking no shortcuts, attention to detail on a *daily* basis and being sure our team understood our mantra:

+++

"When nothing seems to help, I go and look at a stonecutter hammering away at his rock perhaps a hundred times without as much as a crack showing in it. Yet at the hundred and first blow it will split in two, and I know it was not that blow that did it — but all that had gone before." — Jacob Riis

+++

This group of men learned to respect the opportunity, the challenge, each other and our opponents in a quest for the ultimate basketball goal.

Our season did not start smoothly and injuries to Speedy Claxton, Ginobili and Smith aggravated the situation. We persevered, continued to pound away at practice and, very slowly, a personality began to develop. We became quite committed to defense and took great pride in wearing people down in that regard. At the same time our offense became a bit more coordinated between inside and outside. As the All-Star break approached, it was apparent Tim Duncan was even more powerful in play and leadership than the year before and David Robinson was very focused on being ready for a final playoff run. Although injured from time to time, David worked hard and maintained his usual high standard. Our nine game road odyssey in February, where we went 8-1, solidified our rotation with a now healthy Ginobili, Malik Rose and Steve Kerr off the bench, and inspired play by Willis, Smith and Ferry in appropriate matchups. It was clear by now that Jackson, Parker and Ginobili were genuine articles and real competitors. Bruce Bowen, with his yeoman work ethic, turned himself into one of the best three point shooters in the league — what a plus!

As the end of the regular season approached our basketball team was confident and secure in the knowledge of what we had to do to win and they were all willing to make the necessary sacrifices.

The first round of the playoffs was a difficult one as we explored how to play against a young and very talented Phoenix team. It was a growing process for several players in that we faced adversity quickly due to some heroics from our opponent. The wins on the road in Games 3 and 6 were of paramount importance for our confidence and reassurance that what we needed to do was concentrate on how we play and win.

In round two we faced a team we swept for a championship in 1999 and one that made quick work of us the past two seasons. Winning the first two games at home gave us a bit too much comfort as we dropped Games 3 and 4 in Los Angeles. As the series progressed Duncan showed his prowess as the MVP of the 2002-2003 season by elevating his play with each game against Shaquille O'Neal who was intent on stopping him and who had done a good job in the past. In Game 5 and the closing Game 6 in Los Angeles, Tim was breathtaking as he led the squad to victory (another 4-2 series). It had become apparent to all that Tim's teammates were very much capable of handling the situation as we watched Parker, Jackson, Bowen and Ginobili thrill on the perimeter and Rose and Willis fight Shaq and others at every turn in the paint.

In the third round against Dallas, as we expected, would prove to be another type of problem. Our transition defense would be tested as never before and our matchups would cause us particular consternation. We saw the emergence of Parker as a competitor and a winner with Claxton continuing to provide solid and inspired backup. We were truly a deep squad that felt it could accomplish the task at hand. In a 4-2 series victory, we were once again able to win and close on the road, which was a source of great satisfaction for all.

As we prepared for New Jersey, we were quite aware of their 10-0 streak in the playoffs and knew they would not only be confident but quite hungry, having tasted defeat in the NBA Finals versus the Lakers the year before. It would be difficult to match the focus they would bring and much time was spent on the mental approach to this problem. Our players were impressive as they continued their team play at both ends of the court and came up with huge victories in New Jersey in Games 3 and 5. In Game 6 we witnessed another defensive struggle and finally exploded for a 19-0 run that propelled us to a second NBA Championship. Tim Duncan's near quadruple double and Robinson's inspired play allowed others to keep the faith as the final game progressed and the heroics of Ginobili, Claxton and Jackson down the stretch sealed it.

It was a privilege, an honor, and a thrill to be part of what this group accomplished. The coaches congratulate a wonderful team that won with hard work, courage and humility.

The Rock Has Split In Two.

Gregg C. Popovich

DAVID ROBINSON

"This has been the ride of my life. There is no place to celebrate like San Antonio."

NBA
CHAMPIONS

ONE BY ONE, SILVER AND BLACK BARGES STREWNED WITH BASKETBALL BALLOONS, LAZILY MADE THEIR WAY AROUND THE BEND IN THE WORLD FAMOUS RIVERWALK. FANS WEARING THEIR FAVORITE SPURS JERSEYS WAITED FOR HOURS, LINING THE COBBLESTONE WALKWAYS AND ARCHED FOOTBRIDGES OF ERNIE PYLE'S "AMERICAN VENICE," DESPERATE TO GET CLOSE TO THEIR BASKETBALL HEROES. OUTSTRETCHED ARMS SURGED AS FANS ALONG THE BANKS DELICATELY BALANCED THEMSELVES AS THEY THANKED THEIR BELOVED NBA CHAMPIONS WHO FLOATED BY TO A CHORUS OF "GO SPURS GO."

It was a two-in-a-half-mile river of madness as more than 300,000 fans gathered for the SBC 2003 Spurs Championship celebration. In a city that is known for throwing some of the world's most unforgettable parties, this basketball fiesta was unlike any other championship coronation.

"San Antonio throws great parties, and this will be another party to be remembered," said Mayor Ed Garza. It certainly was.

Pennants and homemade signs dotted the masses — *Thanks for the memories, Mr. David Robinson … We love you, Tim* — as kids sat on their father's shoulders, hoping to catch a glimpse of the newest NBA champions.

Soon another boisterous eruption could be heard as chants of Steve Kerr's name echoed from the restaurants, cafes and balconies three stories high as his barge, also containing teammate Danny Ferry, slowly drifted around the bend.

"I want to say thank you to all the fans for coming out today," said Kerr. "You guys are the best. How about a Go Spurs Go chant!"

"Go Spurs Go! Go Spurs Go!"

A member of the Spurs 1999 NBA championship team, Kerr is San Antonio's newest favorite son, who catapulted the Spurs to the NBA Finals with his Game 6 three-point shooting heroics in the Western Conference Finals and followed up that performance with more clutch shooting in the NBA Finals. Undecided on whether he will retire, fans made it quite apparent of their desire as pleas of "Come back, Steve" were heard as his barge slowly floated away to the rocking sounds of the house band.

Another barge made its way, featuring two members of the Spurs' international backcourt, Tony Parker and Manu Ginobili.

"I'm just so happy," said an elated Parker to the adoring crowd. "It's unbelievable. It's like a dream for me. It's just the beginning. We are going to win, like, three or four more."

Ginobili addressed the crowd in both English and Spanish and no doubt he and Parker will return home this summer to Argentina and France to an elevated brand of celebrity.

The parade of barges continued, slowly rolling down the river. Spurs fan and Oscar winner Tommy Lee Jones joined Spurs chairman and CEO Peter Holt as they waved to the crowd while another barge featured students

from Carver Academy, the elementary school David Robinson founded.

Clutching the Larry O'Brien Trophy, Tim Duncan waved to the thousands of fans lined seven rows deep as they greeted him with chants of MVP! MVP!! Standing next to Duncan was Spurs head coach, Gregg Popovich, who addressed the crowd.

"To the best fans in the NBA, we love you," said Popovich. "Thank you for all of your support." Popovich then turned to Duncan and Robinson and said, "What about these two guys right here?" The crowd erupted. After Duncan thanked the Spurs fans, one of the city's most beloved citizens grabbed the microphone.

"This has been the ride of my life," said Robinson, who cleaned out his locker for the final time a day earlier. "There is no place to celebrate like San Antonio. I'm going to be up there in the stands with you all cheering them on next year."

The love fest continued later that evening as 60,000 fans packed the Alamodome to pay homage to the Spurs once again. The crowning moment was a video tribute to Robinson, which featured career highlights, the evolution of his hairstyles as well as testimonials from his teammates and head coach. The delirious capacity crowd saved their loudest cheer for the man who has given the city 14 years of unparalleled dedicated service on and off the court.

"San Antonio, you have the best group of guys in the NBA," said Robinson. "These men, not only can they play basketball, they have character."

The championship journey was especially sweet for veteran forward Kevin Willis, who at 41 years of age and with more than 1,300 games played, clearly basked in the moment.

"I've been in this league 19 years," said Willis, "and this is the biggest and most satisfying time of my career."

For Duncan, who was a member of the 1999 championship team, the second title is just as sweet.

"It was everything it was in '99," said Duncan. "San Antonio fans are so loyal to their teams." 🏀

GREGG POPOVICH *San Antonio Spurs head coach*

"He's our heart and soul out there. We ask him to do everything."

TIM DUNCAN

HE HAS BEEN COMPARED TO SOME OF THE GREATEST LOW-POST PLAYERS IN NBA HISTORY: ABDUL-JABBAR, WALTON, MCHALE. HALL OF FAMER WILLIS REED HAS CALLED HIM THE GREATEST FUNDAMENTAL PLAYER IN THE GAME TODAY. AFTER ONLY SIX NBA SEASONS, TIM DUNCAN IS NOT ONLY COMPILING POINTS, REBOUNDS AND CHAMPIONSHIPS, HE'S RECEIVING THE UTMOST RESPECT REGARDING HIS PLACE ON THE MOUNT RUSHMORE OF BASKETBALL GREATS.

"TIM DUNCAN IS ALREADY ONE OF THE TOP 10 GREATEST PLAYERS IN THE HISTORY OF BASKETBALL," SAID TWO-TIME NBA CHAMPION BILL WALTON. "HE IS THE PETE SAMPRAS OF BASKETBALL. HE'S SO METHODICAL, SO CLASSICALLY TRAINED. HE PUTS HIMSELF IN THE POSITION EVERY SINGLE GAME TO BE THE ULTIMATE WINNER BY MASTERING EVERY SINGLE ASPECT OF THE GAME OF BASKETBALL. IN COMBINING HIS FUNDAMENTAL SKILLS WITH A CRISPLY ANALYTICAL MIND, HE HAS DEVELOPED TO THE POINT WHERE HE IS VIRTUALLY UNBEATABLE."

NBA FINALS MVP MULTIPLE WINNERS

[Award was first issued in 1969]

WILLIS REED *1970, 1973*

KAREEM ABDUL-JABBAR *1971, 1985*

MAGIC JOHNSON *1980, 1982, 1987*

LARRY BIRD *1984, 1986*

MICHAEL JORDAN *1991-93, 1996-98*

HAKEEM OLAJUWON *1994, 1995*

SHAQUILLE O'NEAL *2000-2002*

TIM DUNCAN *1999, 2003*

The praise is certainly justified as Duncan's gaudy basketball résumé sparkles in achievement. The 7-0, 260-pound forward-center led the Spurs to an NBA best 60 regular-season wins and picked up his second straight NBA MVP award, becoming the first player to win back-to-back honors since Michael Jordan did it in 1991 and '92. When the St. Croix native earned his second NBA Finals MVP award in the 2003 NBA Finals, Duncan joined Jordan, Larry Bird and Magic Johnson as the only players in NBA history to win at least two NBA MVPs, two Finals MVPs and an All-Star Game MVP.

Someone who has witnessed greatness on a nightly basis when he was in a Chicago Bulls uniform, says there are similarities between Duncan and Jordan in that they both dominate on a consistent basis.

"They do it in different ways," said Spurs guard Steve Kerr, who played with Jordan on three NBA championship teams with the Bulls. "It was always Michael, and the rest of us trying to help out. It's the same with Tim. It's his game. Like with Michael, they get numbers and you just expect it every game. It's the ultimate sign of how good he is."

Just don't expect Duncan to tell you how great he is. It's not in his personality. In an age of instant gratification and showmanship, the superstar player is a throwback.

"He's not a flair sort of person," said Spurs head coach Gregg Popovich. "He's not an MTV sort of guy. He doesn't beat his chest and point at you. He keeps the same expression. Doesn't matter who he's played against."

Similar to his demeanor, Duncan is workmanlike when it comes to his on-court approach. Bank shots, rebounds, pinpoint passing. Duncan's game clearly emphasizes substance over style.

"Tim Duncan is probably the best big man, as far as his footwork and using his fundamentals," said New Jersey Nets head coach Byron Scott.

The maturation of Duncan as a player also extended to his leadership

> ## "TIM DUNCAN IS PROBABLY THE BEST BIG MAN, AS FAR AS HIS FOOTWORK AND USING HIS FUNDAMENTALS."
>
> BYRON SCOTT *New Jersey Nets head coach*

skills. The reserved All-Star has assert-ed himself more with his teammates, on and off the court.

"As the year progressed, Timmy has become more and more demonstra-tive," said Popovich. "He's really understanding the effect he has on both ends of the court and he's demanding from his teammates. That's a sign when a star steps up to that superstar status. He really understands the effect he has but also the responsi-bility he has to make that happen. He cherishes that responsibility so he's having a really good time with that."

ON A TEAM FEATURING A 21-YEAR-OLD POINT GUARD IN TONY PARKER, A ROOKIE GUARD IN MANU GINOBILI AND A THIRD-YEAR SWINGMAN IN STEPHEN JACKSON, DUNCAN NEEDED TO EXERT HIS EXPERTISE THIS SEASON.

"We've got a young team," said Duncan. "I had to be more of a leader and be more vocal on the court and make every aspect as easy as I can."

Duncan's guidance has paid off. Parker came of age during the red-hot spotlight of the playoffs while Ginobili and Jackson also responded through-out the Spurs' championship run.

"He has confidence in me," said Jackson. "And when you know the NBA MVP has confidence in you, it definitely helps your game."

The evolution of Duncan as a leader also took major strides this sea-son in finding open teammates and having the confidence in their abilities to come through. That was evident throughout the playoffs as teams col-lapsed defensively on him, leaving his teammates open on the perimeter.

"When he is double teamed out on the floor, he had to learn to trust the

Steve Kerrs of the world," said Popovich. "Tim is learning that as well. That's really the evolution of his game and he obviously has great capacity in that area, and without that, we would not be much of a team."

With David Robinson retiring, the legend of great San Antonio players continues with Duncan as he faces the challenge of winning more NBA titles.

"The way Tim is playing, he's at his prime and is going to contin-ue to play great," said Robinson. "The team definitely has potential to stay right where they are. There's no question."

"TIMMY, HE'S A GREAT PLAYER. HE'S OUR MVP."

TONY PARKER

CONSECUTIVE SEASON NBA MVP AWARD WINNERS

BILL RUSSELL, 3
[1960-61, 1961-62, 1962-63]

WILT CHAMBERLAIN, 3
[1965-66, 1966-67, 1967-68]

KAREEM ABDUL-JABBAR, 2
[1975-76, 1976-77]

MOSES MALONE, 2
[1981-82, 1982-83]

LARRY BIRD, 3
[1983-84, 1984-85, 1985-86]

MAGIC JOHNSON, 2
[1988-89, 1989-90]

MICHAEL JORDAN, 2
[1990-91, 1991-92]

TIM DUNCAN, 2
[2001-02, 2002-03]

GREGG POPOVICH *San Antonio Spurs head coach*

"I'm going to most miss the kind of person he is, his presence, the disposition he brings to practice and games and trips, the class he exudes. I'm going to miss that more than anything because I think he makes a statement for our club, and it's a standard everyone tries to meet that most of us can't."

DAVID ROBINSON

THE LIST OF ON-COURT ACCOMPLISHMENTS ARE IMPECCABLE. DURING 14 NBA SEA-SONS, DAVID ROBINSON SET A STANDARD OF EXCELLENCE FEW PLAYERS IN THE HISTORY OF THE GAME CAN MATCH. THE FORMER NAVAL OFFICER IS ONE OF THE MOST DECORATED PLAYERS IN LEAGUE HISTORY HAVING WON VIRTUALLY EVERY AWARD IMAGINABLE. DURING HIS FIRST SEVEN SEASONS ALONE, ROBINSON ESTABLISHED HIMSELF AS ONE OF THE GAME'S ALL-TIME GREAT CENTERS, WIN-NING THE NBA ROOKIE OF THE YEAR AWARD, A REBOUNDING TITLE, A SCORING CHAMPIONSHIP, A MOST VALUABLE PLAYER AWARD, DEFENSIVE PLAYER OF THE YEAR HONORS, SEVEN ALL-STAR APPEARANCES, NOT TO MENTION FOUR ALL-NBA FIRST TEAM AND NBA ALL-DEFENSIVE FIRST TEAM SELECTIONS.

YET IT WAS THE ARRIVAL OF TIM DUNCAN IN 1997 THAT WOULD EVENTUALLY HELP ROBINSON FULFILL HIS BIGGEST GOAL, WINNING AN NBA CHAMPIONSHIP.

"**O**ne of the things about this league is that you have to know who you are," said Robinson who was named one of the 50 Greatest Players in NBA History in 1996. "For my first eight years I spent a lot of time trying to figure out how to make this team better. But I've never been a Michael Jordan-type of player. Having Tim let me find my own place and get us to the next level."

That next level meant Robinson scoring less and allowing Duncan to blossom into a two-time NBA MVP. Despite

Robinson's impressive basketball résumé, it was a role he easily embraced.

"Right from the get-go, I knew his talent was going to be on the offensive end of the basket," said Robinson, who has played on three U.S. Olympic teams. "Everybody talks about me sacrificing my game, I didn't really think I was sacrificing my game. I just thought if we want to win, this is the way we need to play. As the years have gone on, he's gotten better and better and our team has gotten better and better."

NOT ONLY DID ROBINSON RECOGNIZE THE TALENT IN DUNCAN BUT HE TOOK THE OPPORTUNITY TO MENTOR THE 21-YEAR-OLD ROOKIE AS WELL.

"The veterans that were around when I was starting out weren't very vocal," said Robinson, who was the No. 1 overall pick in the 1987 NBA Draft. "I had Terry Cummings, Maurice Cheeks and Caldwell Jones on my team. They were kind of quiet. It's nice for young guys to have someone to talk to about this lifestyle, so I make myself available if they want it."

This approach was welcomed and appreciated by Duncan who couldn't ask for a better mentor or situation upon entering the NBA.

"The great thing about him is that he never forced himself upon me. He never said, 'Hey, this is how you do it' or 'This is the way I want you to do it.' He would always say 'I'm here if you have a question' and 'I'm here if you want to learn something.' That was really great about him."

"HE IS TRULY A CLASS GUY AND A GREAT
REPRESENTATIVE FOR HIS TEAM AND
THE LEAGUE. I ADMIRE HIM GREATLY."

RUDY TOMJANOVICH
former Houston Rockets coach

DAVID ROBINSON

"I'M SO MUCH OF AN IN-THE-MOMENT, TODAY TYPE OF PERSON. I THINK THAT'S WHAT MAKES ME HAPPY. ONE OF MY FAVORITE [BIBLICAL] VERSES IS MATTHEW 6:34: 'DO NOT WORRY ABOUT TOMORROW FOR TODAY HAS ENOUGH TROUBLE OF ITS OWN.'"

The team's success has made them the most successful twin-towers' duo in NBA history. In six seasons, the Duncan-Robinson tandem produced two NBA titles while also recording the NBA's best regular-season record in three of those seasons.

Although Robinson's on-court accomplishments loom large, his greatest legacy has nothing to do with the number of championships or points scored. It is his philanthropic efforts off the court that have people inspired.

"Last summer, I was taking my daughter to look at colleges," said Spurs owner Peter Holt. "We were in North Carolina, at Duke, and they were taking us around, you know how they do. Someone heard that we were from San Antonio, and the first thing they said was that they always admired David Robinson. I think my daughter mentioned something about us being involved in the team and they got excited and just begged us, 'Will you tell David Robinson that we really admire him so much?'

"Young kids these days, they want Allen Iverson and all of that, but these people they really wanted to talk about David Robinson. There are lots of people out there who truly respect and believe in that man as I do."

Robinson is a giant in the San Antonio community, admired for his long-standing commitment of reaching out to young people. Through the David Robinson Foundation, the 10-time All-Star donated $9 million dollars toward the construction and operation of the independent Carver Academy, an elementary school for students from a culturally diverse community located east of downtown San Antonio. The Christian based school offers elementary-age children a challenging academ-ic program featuring small classes, leadership opportunities, and a nurturing family-like environment based upon the foundation of Judeo-Christian scripture. Named for George Washington Carver, the school opened on September 17, 2001 with 60 pre-kindergarten through second grade children. The Carver Academy added a third grade class in 2002. The school's goal is to eventually accommodate up to 290 students through eighth grade. Already the results are encouraging. Last year, Carver Academy students scored above the national average of 50, establishing a mark of 70.

"These are all my kids," said Robinson, who plans on raising donations for the school in his retirement. "In 20 years, you are going to see these kids come out and change not just the community, but change the world."

During the NBA Finals, the NBA dedicated its 60th Reading and Learning Center to Carver Academy, providing the school with thousands of donated books along with resource guides and materials

"HE HAS SET THE STANDARD FOR COMMUNITY INVOLVEMENT BY AN ATHLETE."

DAVID STERN *NBA Commissioner*

in addition to computers, printers and educational software.

"David Robinson's legacy," said NBA Commissioner David Stern, "is one of intensity and competitiveness in basketball, balanced with a great ability off the court to recognize how important he could be to his community."

Robinson, for whom the league renamed its monthly community assist award — The David Robinson Plaque — is thrilled with the school's impact on the children.

"LIFE IS NOT JUST ABOUT THAT BASKETBALL GOING IN THE HOOP," SAID ROBINSON, WHO RECEIVED THE J. WALTER KENNEDY AWARD THIS SEASON FOR OUTSTANDING COMMUNITY SERVICE. "IT'S ABOUT OTHER THINGS. WHEN I GET TO THIS SCHOOL AND SEE THESE YOUNG KIDS AND THE IMPACT WE CAN HAVE IN THEIR LIVES, IT'S PHENOMENAL."

Robinson retires from the game the way all professional athletes dream of retiring — on top. Although you get a sense when you hear him speak that success isn't merely defined by the number of individual accolades or championships. There is a bigger picture to consider, a much more valuable one in his mind as he looks ahead.

"It's funny, when I think about my career, I don't think I deserve any more credit than what I've gotten," Robinson said. "It's been pretty fun. In the long run, it's not so much what people say about you, it's what you left behind. You know, the impact you've had on people's lives. I've had some great opportunities getting to know some guys and be a part of their lives, so it's been fun. That's what makes my career a success more than anything."

"HE'S A VERY DEAR FRIEND. WE'VE ALWAYS HAD FUN BEING AROUND EACH OTHER. EVEN AFTER BASKETBALL, I'LL CONSIDER HIM A FRIEND."

TIM DUNCAN

REGULAR SEASON CAREER STATS

SEASON	G	Min.	FGM	FGA	Pct.	FTM	FTA	Pct.	REBOUNDS Off.	Def.	Total	Ast.	St.	Blk.	TO	Pts.	AVERAGES RPG	APG	PPG
87-88 DNP - Military Service																			
88-89 DNP - Military Service																			
89-90	82	3002	690	1300	.531	613	837	.732	303	680	983	164	138	319	257	1993	12.0	2.0	24.3
90-91	82	3095	754	1366	.552	592	777	.762	335	728	1063	208	127	320	270	2101	13.0	2.5	25.6
91-92	68	2564	592	1074	.551	393	561	.701	261	568	829	181	158	305	182	1578	12.2	2.7	23.2
92-93	82	3211	676	1348	.501	561	766	.732	229	727	956	301	127	264	241	1916	11.7	3.7	23.4
93-94	80	3241	840	1658	.507	693	925	.749	241	614	855	381	139	265	253	2383	10.7	4.8	29.8
94-95	81	3074	788	1487	.530	656	847	.774	234	643	877	236	134	262	233	2238	10.8	2.9	27.6
95-96	82	3019	711	1378	.516	626	823	.761	319	681	1000	247	111	271	190	2051	12.2	3.0	25.0
96-97	6	147	36	72	.500	34	52	.654	19	32	51	8	6	6	8	106	8.5	1.3	17.7
97-98	73	2457	544	1065	.511	485	660	.735	239	536	775	199	64	192	202	1574	10.6	2.7	21.6
98-99	49	1554	268	527	.509	239	363	.658	148	344	492	103	69	119	108	775	10.0	2.1	15.8
99-00	80	2557	528	1031	.512	371	511	.726	193	577	770	142	97	183	164	1427	9.6	1.8	17.8
00-01	80	2371	400	823	.486	351	470	.747	208	483	691	116	80	197	122	1151	8.6	1.5	14.4
01-02	78	2303	341	672	.507	269	395	.681	191	456	647	94	86	140	104	951	8.3	1.2	12.2
02-03	64	1676	197	420	.469	152	214	.710	163	345	508	61	52	111	83	546	7.9	1.0	8.5
Totals	987	34271	7365	14221	.518	6035	8201	.736	3083	7414	10497	2441	1388	2954	2417	20790	10.6	2.5	21.1

DAVID MAURICE ROBINSON | *Born: August 6, 1965 in Key West, Fla.* | *Height: 7-1* | *Weight: 250 lbs.* | *College: Navy* **NBA MVP** *[1995]* **NBA DEFENSIVE PLAYER OF THE YEAR** *[1992]* **NBA ROOKIE OF THE YEAR** *[1990]* **IBM AWARD,** *for all-around contributions to team's success [1990, 1991, 1994, 1995, 1996]* **NBA SPORTSMANSHIP AWARD** *[2001]* **J. WALTER KENNEDY CITIZENSHIP AWARD** *[2003]* **ALL-NBA FIRST TEAM** *[1991, 1992, 1995, 1996]* **ALL-NBA SECOND TEAM** *[1994, 1998]* **ALL-NBA THIRD TEAM** *[1990, 1993, 2000, 2001]* **NBA ALL-DEFENSIVE FIRST TEAM** *[1991, 1992, 1995, 1996]* **NBA ALL-DEFENSIVE SECOND TEAM** *[1990, 1993, 1994, 1998]* **10-TIME ALL-STAR** *[1990-1996, 1998, 2000, 2001]* **NBA ALL-ROOKIE TEAM** *[1990]* **MEMBER OF NBA CHAMPIONSHIP TEAM** *[1999, 2003]* **MEMBER OF GOLD-MEDAL-WINNING U.S. OLYMPIC TEAMS** *[1992, 1996];* **BRONZE-MEDAL-WINNING U.S. OLYMPIC TEAM** *[1988]*

PLAYOFF CAREER STATS

SEASON	G	Min.	FGM	FGA	Pct.	FTM	FTA	Pct.	REBOUNDS Off.	Def.	Total	Ast.	St.	Blk.	TO	Pts.	AVERAGES RPG	APG	PPG
89-90	10	375	89	167	.533	65	96	.677	36	84	120	23	11	40	24	243	12.0	2.3	24.3
90-91	4	166	35	51	.686	33	38	.868	11	43	54	8	6	15	15	103	13.5	2.0	25.8
92-93	10	421	79	170	.465	73	110	.664	29	97	126	40	10	36	25	231	12.6	4.0	23.1
93-94	4	146	30	73	.411	20	27	.741	13	27	40	14	3	10	9	80	10.0	3.5	20.0
94-95	15	623	129	289	.446	121	149	.812	57	125	182	47	22	39	56	380	12.1	3.1	25.3
95-96	10	353	83	161	.516	70	105	.667	37	64	101	24	15	25	24	236	10.1	2.4	23.6
97-98	9	353	57	134	.425	61	96	.635	41	86	127	23	11	30	25	175	14.1	2.6	19.4
98-99	17	600	87	180	.483	91	126	.722	36	132	168	43	28	40	40	265	9.9	2.5	15.6
99-00	4	155	31	83	.373	32	42	.762	17	38	55	10	7	12	8	94	13.8	2.5	23.5
00-01	13	409	75	159	.472	66	95	.695	39	114	153	22	17	31	28	216	11.8	1.7	16.6
01-02	4	81	9	19	.474	0	4	.000	6	17	23	5	3	3	2	18	5.8	1.3	4.5
02-03	23	539	64	118	.542	52	78	.667	45	107	152	21	18	31	24	180	6.6	.9	7.8
Totals	123	4221	768	1604	.479	684	966	.708	367	934	1301	280	151	312	280	2221	10.6	2.3	18.1

He's in charge and you don't forget that as a coach. He will yell at Tim, he will yell at Dave. He says what needs to be said and he's not afraid to do that. I can't say that about every coach that I've ever played for and that's very important in the NBA because when the younger guys see him getting on Tim and Dave, they know that they can't get away with much either."

GREGG
POPOVICH

THE NBA COACHING ELITE IS AN EXCLUSIVE FRATERNITY. ITS MEMBERSHIP STANDARDS ARE EXTREMELY STRINGENT. ONLY A SELECT GROUP OF MEN IN THE NBA'S 57-YEAR HISTORY HAVE EARNED THE COVETED DISTINCTION OF WINNING TWO OR MORE TITLES IN THEIR CAREERS. THE HIGH-PROFILE CLUB FEATURES THE LIKES OF RED AUERBACH, PHIL JACKSON, JOHN KUNDLA, RED HOLZMAN, PAT RILEY AND CHUCK DALY, AMONG OTHERS, AND RECENTLY WELCOMED ITS NEWEST MEMBER, GREGG POPOVICH.

The U.S. Air Force Academy graduate gained entry by becoming only the 12th coach in NBA history to win two or more titles after the San Antonio Spurs put the finishing touches on the New Jersey Nets in Game 6 of the 2003 NBA Finals. It is an honor that is accepted with a great deal of humility.

"I still wake up wondering, 'What the hell am I doing here?'" said Popovich. "I think every day is a blessing and a picnic, and I'm waiting for it to end."

Coaching success is a touchy subject for Popovich, one that is clearly a source of discomfort. Watching him accept the Red Auerbach Trophy for the 2003 NBA Coach of the Year was indicative of his self-effacing approach. As he addressed the media, it was quite evident the last place he wanted to be was at a podium accepting the league's highest coaching honor

"There are a whole lot of people who could be standing here," said Popovich. "It's almost embarrassing

in a sense. I just happen to have a good group around me."

Popovich, who guided the Spurs to a league best 60-22 record and a Midwest Division title, wasn't finished deflecting the spotlight.

"A few years ago we won the No. 1 pick in the lottery. If we hadn't gotten [Tim] Duncan, who thinks Popovich would be standing here?"

It isn't quite that simple. Without a doubt, having the two-time NBA MVP and perhaps the most fundamentally sound player in the league

on your roster doesn't hurt, but it takes more than Duncan to have the success Popovich has enjoyed during the last seven seasons. Thanks to Popovich the general manager, the Spurs were successfully rebuilt twice in four years, resulting in two NBA championships. Only Duncan, David Robinson, Steve Kerr and Malik Rose remained from the 1999 championship team.

The 54-year-old has established an impressive résumé since he assumed the coaching duties on December 10, 1996. This past season saw Popovich become the ninth fastest coach in NBA history to record his 300th victory

and he currently ranks as the Spurs all-time leader with a 339-185 record. Under Popovich's guidance, the Spurs have won three straight Midwest Division titles and he pulled a rare double double this season, joining Auerbach, Holzman, Bill Sharman and Jackson as the only coaches to win NBA Coach of the Year and an NBA title in the same season.

The path to NBA coaching elite began at the Air Force Academy, where Popovich served as an assistant coach for six seasons before moving on to Pomona-Pitzer, a Division III college in Claremont, Calif. During his eight seasons, Popovich led his team to the school's first conference championship in 68 years. In 1988, he joined Larry Brown as a Spurs assistant coach where he spent four seasons before moving on to join Don Nelson in Golden State. In 1994, Popovich became the Spurs Executive Vice President of Basketball Operations and General Manager and took over the coaching responsibilities after 18 games during the 1996-97 season.

Since then, Popovich has ruled with a firm but flexible hand and his ability to find and develop young talent such as Tony Parker and Manu Ginobili has paid huge dividends. Popovich, who turned over the GM duties to R.C. Buford last summer, also demonstrated his ability to connect with free-spirited players such as Stephen Jackson.

"I think Pop is probably the only one who can control me," said Jackson. "I know a lot of times my emotions can go the wrong way, but Pop helps me control that. I think I need to be around Pop because he makes me a better player."

It's a common characteristic that all elite coaches possess. ♨

NBA COACHING ELITE
[Coaches who have won 2 or more NBA titles]

RED AUERBACH, 9
Boston ('57,'59 –'66)
938 W | 479 L | .662 PCT

PHIL JACKSON, 9
Chicago / L.A ('91–'93,'96–'98,'00–'02)
776 W | 290 L | .728 PCT

JOHN KUNDLA, 5
Minneapolis ('49–'50, '52–'54)
423 W | 302 L | .583 PCT

PAT RILEY, 4
L.A ('82, '85,'87–'88)
1110 W | 569 L | .661 PCT

CHUCK DALY, 2
Detroit ('89–'90)
638 W | 437 L | .593 PCT

ALEX HANNUM, 2
St. Louis / Philadelphia ('58,'67)
471 W | 412 L | .533 PCT

TOM HEINSOHN, 2
Boston ('74,'76)
427 W | 263 L | .619 PCT

RED HOLZMAN, 2
New York ('70,'73)
696 W | 604 L | .535 PCT

K.C. JONES, 2
Boston ('84,'86)
522 W | 252 L | .674 PCT

GREGG POPOVICH, 2
San Antonio ('99,'03)
339 W | 185 L | .647 PCT

BILL RUSSELL, 2
Boston ('68–'69)
341 W | 290 L | .540 PCT

RUDY TOMJANOVICH, 2
Houston ('94–'95)
503 W | 397 L | .559 PCT

TIM DUNCAN

"Guys have really been ready to play off our bench, and that's something that's been great for us. They are ready to go. They are at the call and ready for every game."

TEAM

THE CHAMPIONSHIP MISSION WAS FAR FROM OVER BUT GREGG POPOVICH TOOK A WELL DESERVED MOMENT FOLLOWING THE SPURS' GAME 6 ELIMINATION OF THE LOS ANGELES LAKERS IN THE WESTERN CONFERENCE SEMIFINALS TO REFLECT ON HIS TEAM'S RAPID GROWTH. IT WAS A CANDID ASSESSMENT, ONE THAT REVEALED THE CONCERNS AND QUESTIONS REGARDING KEY PERSONNEL THAT LINGERED FROM TRAINING CAMP THROUGHOUT THE REGULAR SEASON.

"At the beginning of the year, we didn't know what Stephen Jackson was going to be," said Popovich. "We didn't know if he was going to make the team, if he was going to play a lot for us. We didn't know if we were right about Manu [Ginobili]. He had to prove himself.

"Tony Parker was in his sophomore year and oftentimes that's not good for a guy. They surprise people at first, but sometimes after that it doesn't work out. It's David's last year, [and] we didn't know how healthy he would be.

"As the season went on, we expected more and more from them so there is no surprise now that we're playing the way we're playing. But if you take it back to the first day of training camp and say this is going to happen, I would have said, 'Well, you know, you're getting a bit ahead of yourself. A lot, maybe.'"

Try more than a lot. It was unlikely at the start of the season that anyone would have predicted the Spurs winning the NBA championship, not with the myriad of questions that Popovich outlined. Who would have imagined a starting backcourt featuring a 20-year-old point guard in Parker, the last pick of the first round of the 2001 NBA Draft, and a 24-year-old shooting guard in Jackson, who was cut from three different NBA teams, leading the Spurs to the promised land? Or Ginobili, the 57th pick of the 1999 draft, being one of the most athletic players on the court, routinely making key steals, delivering breathtaking behind-the-back passes and finishing breaks with a flourish? What about Bruce Bowen leading the NBA in three-point shooting percentage in addition to his stifling

defense? Or Speedy Claxton, a player who has missed more games than he has played in his young career, providing the Spurs with a lift off the bench during the most crucial stretches of a game?

Somehow, everything fell into place for San Antonio whose mix of talented, athletic and inexperienced players emphatically answered any and all questions throughout the playoffs. It was a team in which new heroes emerged on a nightly basis to complement the all-around brilliance of two-time NBA MVP Tim Duncan. Parker ... Bowen ... Jackson ...Ginobili ... Rose ... Kerr ... Claxton ... Ferry ... Willis. Everyone played a co-starring role, including the Admiral, David Robinson, in San Antonio's championship season.

It was largely a group of overlooked players carefully scouted and hand picked by Popovich and R.C. Buford,

GO SPURS GO

the team's General Manager. The first bold move by Popovich was inserting Parker as the team's starting point guard just five games into his rookie season in 2001-02. The player who played professionally in France responded to this crash course of on-the-job training, averaging 9.2 points and 4.3 assists per game, while also earning NBA All-Rookie First Team honors. More was expected of Parker in his second season and he certainly responded, emerging as one of the NBA's most improved players. Parker averaged 15.5 points and 5.3 assists per game. Popovich has been instrumental in the recently turned 21-year-old's rapid development over the last two seasons, adopting a tough love approach to his basketball prodigy.

"Tony and I have a relationship where I always tell him that I don't care if he's 20, I want him to play like he's 32."

More often than not, he has.

After stops in the CBA, Europe, the Miami Heat (twice), the Boston Celtics and Philadelphia 76ers, Bruce Bowen learned early on that his ticket to NBA success would be through his defense. The man who grew up in Fresno, Calif., had one of the best role models to reference: former Laker Michael Cooper. Now, Bowen has earned the reputation as one of the NBA's premier versatile defensive players after curtailing some of the league's top scorers. This season he was named to the NBA's All-Defensive Second Team.

"He's an animal," said Robinson.

Tenacious defense isn't the only aspect of Bowen's game. The 6-7 small forward, who took a public relations course at the University of Texas at San Antonio during the season to pursue his degree, also became one of the NBA's premier three-point shooters, making 44 percent of his attempts during the season.

The man who goes by the name of "Jack" because of two other Steves on the team (Kerr and Smith), took a well-traveled road before finally finding a home in San Antonio. Drafted by the Phoenix Suns in 1997, Stephen Jackson's basketball résumé consisted of visits to three NBA training camps, two CBA teams and two pro ball tours of duty in the Dominican Republic and Venezuela — all in a span of three seasons.

The 6-8, 220-pound swingman joined the Spurs last season and has blossomed this season in his role as the team's starting shooting guard.

"I learned how to be a professional here," said Jackson. "There's no egos on this team. It's just down-to-earth guys who love basketball and are good people. That's why I fit in so well here."

How valuable is Malik Rose to the Spurs? The Spurs' sixth man serves as a barometer for the team's success. When he plays well, the team usually wins, which is quite often, evidenced by their NBA best 60 regular-season wins. The 6-7, 255-pound forward is a relentless worker who poses problems for players much bigger than him. Rose averaged 10.4 points and 6.4 rebounds in 24.5 minutes of action during the regular season and provided a lift for most of the playoffs, especially in the first round, when he averaged 13.8 points and 8.7 rebounds against the Phoenix Suns.

Back home in Argentina, Manu Ginobili isn't considered merely a valuable role player, rather he's treated as a conquering hero. Throughout the playoffs, Ginobili's name was splashed across the front pages of Argentina's leading newspapers: *Phenomenal!*, *Super Manu Guided San Antonio* and *The Spurs of Ginobili*. The treatment is significant, especially in the soccer-crazed country where superstar status is reserved only for the elite players. The 6-6 shooting guard, who helped lead Argentina to a silver medal in the World Championship, wasn't able to show the San Antonio fans what all the fuss was about earlier in the season due to an ankle injury he suffered in the tournament. The injury lingered for the first few months of the

"TONY AND I HAVE A RELATIONSHIP WHERE I ALWAYS TELL HIM THAT I DON'T CARE IF HE'S 20, I WANT HIM TO PLAY LIKE HE'S 32."

GREGG POPOVICH

season but when he was finally 100 percent, he infused the Spurs with instant energy off the bench. Energy that translated into big-time results.

"I knew when he got healthy, we were really going to be something," said Robinson. "Manu, he's kind of taken our team to another level. Sometimes, he startles me on the bench — he's making those unbelievable passes, and we're jumping up and down."

Nick Van Exel calls Steve Kerr the zone buster and for good reason. The 6-3, 185-pound guard is one of the most feared three-point shooters in the game. Although he averaged less than 13 minutes and four points per game during the regular season, Kerr was huge for the Spurs when called upon during the postseason. In Game 6 of the Western Conference Finals, Kerr rescued the Spurs from a 13-point deficit with less than 11 minutes remaining and nailed four three-pointers during San Antonio's amazing 23-0 run. Thanks to his heroics, the Spurs advanced to the NBA Finals. Kerr also played an invaluable role in San Antonio's Game 5 NBA Finals victory against the New Jersey Nets.

"He hasn't stopped practicing every day, even though he hasn't played," said Popovich. "Practicing, working, working. He's always ready."

Speedy Claxton was acquired with little fanfare during the offseason to add point guard depth. The player out of Hofstra University, who suffered a torn ACL and missed his entire rookie season with the Philadelphia 76ers, did more than just spell Parker at point, he often took over whenever

the 21-year-old took a breather. When healthy, Claxton played a valuable role throughout the season but really stepped up in the Spurs' Game 5 and Game 6 victories of the Finals.

"Speedy's gotten us through while Tony's been deciding how aggressive he was going to be or how hard he was going to play," said Popovich. "He's done a great job."

For Kevin Willis, Steve Smith and Danny Ferry, the road to the NBA Finals was a long and winding one. The three veterans played a combined 3,080 regular-season games before reaching basketball's biggest stage. Willis

and Smith even ranked eighth and 11th respectively in playoff games played (85 and 80) without reaching the Finals.

"I thought I'd be here long before this," said Willis. "I had no idea. It just teaches you to love the moment, that's what it does."

The players combined for nearly 13 points in 41 minutes of action and performed a valuable role off the bench, which also included 6-11 center Mengke Bateer. Acquired prior to the season, Bateer played in 12 games averaging 3.8 minutes per outing.

It was this collective effort from the supporting cast that was critical in the Spurs fulfilling their championship quest.

STEVE KERR *on the SBC Center*

It gets louder here. It's a basketball gym.
It's not a big football stadium with curtains up."

SEASON

THE REGULAR-SEASON JOURNEY BEGAN WHERE THE SPURS CHAMPIONSHIP HOPES
AND DREAMS ENDED THE LAST TWO SEASONS — IN LOS ANGELES. THE STAPLES
CENTER HAS SERVED AS A CRUEL HOST TO THE SPURS, WHO HAD WON ONLY THREE
TIMES AGAINST THE LAKERS IN 10 PREVIOUS VISITS. THE THREE-YEAR-OLD BUILD-
ING WAS A COLD REMINDER OF EARLY SUMMER VACATIONS AND CHAMPIONSHIP
POTENTIAL UNFULFILLED. THE SPURS WERE DETERMINED TO SET A DIFFERENT
TONE THIS SEASON AND THERE WAS NO BETTER PLACE TO BEGIN THAN AGAINST
THEIR PLAYOFF NEMESIS, THE THREE-TIME DEFENDING NBA CHAMPIONS.

The Lakers were without their superstar center Shaquille O'Neal, who was sidelined with a toe injury, and the Spurs took advantage, winning 87-82. However, it wasn't an impressive victory for San Antonio as Tim Duncan and Tony Parker shot a combined 3 for 24 from the field while the team shot only 36 percent from the floor. It was the Spurs bench that came to the rescue. Reserves Speedy Claxton and rookie Manu Ginobili combined for 20 points, seven assists and six steals.

"It was nice to get the season started off on a right note and to win here," Spurs forward Malik Rose said. "With or without Shaq, I'll take this one. We needed it."

The game served as an indicator of the inconsistency that lied ahead for San Antonio. While their Midwest Division rival Dallas Mavericks stormed to a 14-0 regular-season start, the Spurs sputtered, dealing with an assortment of injuries to players Steve Smith, Claxton and Ginobili. The Spurs also struggled with their free throw shooting and their inability to control the ball, which resulted in too many turnovers. The standings reflected their troubles. The Spurs posted a 9-5 record in their first 14 games and were 19-13 by the end of December. It was an uneven start to the season that

ushered in a new home, the SBC Center and was the final goodbye to an NBA legend, David Robinson, who announced he would set sail to the sparkling NBA retirement waters following the 2002-03 campaign.

The New Year brought renewed optimism as the Spurs showed steady improvement in seizing control of their season. Tim Duncan, who earned NBA Player of the Week honors during the last two weeks of December, was on a roll, averaging nearly 30 points, 14 rebounds, five assists and four blocks per game. Tony Parker, the team's 20-year-old point guard improved his averages across the board, demonstrating newfound confidence while growing into his role as a team leader. When he wasn't raining threes, Bruce Bowen was clamping down on the opponent's top scorer while Stephen Jackson settled in as the team's starting shooting guard. The reserves led by Rose and Ginobili were improving upon their first half numbers, providing a spark off the bench. Everything was clicking as the Spurs went 11-3 in January. Gregg Popovich, who earned NBA Coach of the Month honors, picked up his 300th career victory on January 5 against the Los Angeles Clippers.

The team, which ranked last in free throw shooting, now was close to 80 percent during the stretch while the number of turnovers decreased slightly to around 16 per game.

"They really are a great team, and well-coached," Phoenix guard Stephon Marbury said about the Spurs after they defeated the Suns 108-100 in overtime on January 14. "Tim Duncan is a monster for them. They have a system that they stick by, and they do it well. Everyone on that team knows their

role, and that is definitely why they are a playoff team."

While the Spurs recorded a 26-15 record at the season's half-way point, the true test awaited as the team was set to embark on a nine-game, 23-day road trip, the longest in franchise history, courtesy of the San Antonio Stock Show & Rodeo that rolled into the SBC Center.

After losing the opener to Minnesota, 106-95, the Spurs responded by winning eight straight games, which included victories over Orlando, Portland, the Lakers and Sacramento.

"We knew coming into this road trip how long it was, and this has been a great time for our team to get a personality," said Duncan. "I think that we really have grown and shown a lot of character."

The Spurs gelled during their nearly three-plus week, 11,360 mile odyssey of hostile environments. It provided the team a tremendous confidence booster and springboard for the remainder of the season.

The Spurs' torrid pace resulted in a 9-1 record in February followed by a 14-3 mark in March. Popovich once again earned NBA Coach of the Month honors while Ginobili earned got milk? Rookie of the Month honors. The once untouchable Mavericks were now well within striking distance.

"San Antonio is playing on a very high level," said Mavericks coach Don Nelson with five games remaining. "It looks like nobody's going to beat them. We're going to have to do it in that last game of the season. But for that game to mean something, we're going to have to continue to win."

The Spurs finished the month of April with a 7-2 record, which included a loss against the Mavericks on the last day of the regular season. Both teams finished with identical 60-22 records but San Antonio won the tie-breaker by virtue of owning the better conference record. It was quite a finish for the Spurs, who went 41-9 in their last 50 games as Duncan earned his second consecutive NBA MVP award.

"I'm proud of the team, but it's just beginning," said Parker. "We're going to make a run for it. Our goal is not to win the conference or get the No. 1 seed, it's to win the championship."

STEPHEN JACKSON

"We know what our goal is. Our goal is not to win our division. Our goal is not to win the No. 1 seed. Our goal is to win the Championship. We still have a lot of work to do."

NBA PLAYOFFS

THEY WERE ONE OF THE MOST FEARED TEAMS ENTERING THE NBA PLAYOFFS AND WITH GOOD REASON. SINCE JANUARY 1, NO ONE HAS BEEN HOTTER OR MORE CONVINCING IN ROLLING THROUGH ITS COMPETITION THAN THE SAN ANTONIO SPURS. SIMILAR TO A RUNAWAY LOCOMOTIVE, THE SILVER AND BLACK EXPRESS GAINED MOMENTUM AT EACH TURN — JANUARY 11-3, FEBRUARY 9-1, MARCH 14-3 AND APRIL 7-2 — AND WHEN IT FINALLY PULLED INTO THE NBA PLAYOFFS STATION, THE SPURS HAD COMPILED AN IMPRESSIVE 41-9 RECORD. THE FOUR-MONTH RUN RESULTED IN AN NBA BEST 60-22 MARK, WHICH INCLUDED 18 WINS IN THEIR LAST 20 ROAD GAMES. YET, DESPITE THIS DOMINANCE, MANY QUESTIONS LINGERED. COULD THE SPURS' SUPPORTING CAST, WHICH FEATURED UNTESTED PLAYOFF PERFORMERS TONY PARKER, MANU GINOBILI AND STEPHEN JACKSON, SUSTAIN A NEARLY TWO-MONTH JOURNEY IN PURSUIT OF THE 16 COVETED WINS NECESSARY TO WIN THE LARRY O'BRIEN TROPHY? WOULD A TEAM THAT RANKED NEARLY LAST IN FREE THROW SHOOTING AND TURNOVERS BE ABLE TO OVERCOME THESE DEFICIENCIES IN THE MOST HOSTILE, PRESSURE PACKED ENVIRONMENTS?

THESE QUESTIONS WOULD SOON BE ANSWERED DURING FOUR ROUNDS OF INTENSE COMPETITION VERSUS THE NBA'S BEST TEAMS: PHOENIX SUNS, LOS ANGELES LAKERS, DALLAS MAVERICKS AND NEW JERSEY NETS.

WESTERN CONFERENCE FIRST ROUND

GAME 1, *April 19, 2003*
Phoenix Suns, 96
San Antonio Spurs, 95 (OT)

GAME 2, *April 21, 2003*
San Antonio Spurs, 84
Phoenix Suns, 76

GAME 3, *April 25, 2003*
San Antonio Spurs, 99
Phoenix Suns, 86

GAME 4, *April 27, 2003*
Phoenix Suns, 86
San Antonio Spurs, 84

GAME 5, *April 29, 2003*
San Antonio Spurs, 94
Phoenix Suns, 82

GAME 6, *May 1, 2003*
San Antonio Spurs, 87
Phoenix Suns, 85

On paper, this first-round playoff matchup was a mere formality. The 60-22 San Antonio Spurs, owners of the best regular-season record in the NBA and the top seed in the Western Conference versus the 44-38, eighth-seeded Phoenix Suns. Mere formality, right? Wrong. The Suns had San Antonio's number throughout the regular-season, winning three out of four contests and were looking to translate that success into postseason bliss. They almost did. Stephon Marbury, the Suns' All-Star point guard, banked a three-pointer at the overtime buzzer in Game 1 to send the 19,217 fans at the SBC Center in utter shock.

"That shot was a teardrop from God," Marbury said. "Things were getting tough, but I didn't stop shooting. We never gave up, we never got ourselves into a situation where we'd panic."

The Spurs rebounded in Game 2 to tie the series and Tony Parker, who had struggled against Marbury in the first two games, bounced back with 29 points in the Spurs' Game 3 victory.

The sun appeared to be setting on Phoenix as they trailed the series 2-1 and were staring at a 12-point deficit in the fourth quarter of Game 4. But the Spurs' regular-season nemesis — turnovers — haunted them once again as they have done all season long. The Suns made a valiant comeback, tying the game and eventually winning it on a Jake Voskuhl hook shot.

"That was my first game-winner," said Voskuhl. "Going in to San Antonio [down] 3-1 would have been a really difficult situation. We needed this one and we stepped up."

It was now a best two out of three series and the underdog Suns liked their chances.

"The series is even again with three games left to play and we still haven't played our best game yet," Marbury said. "We still haven't clicked it in yet. They threw their best punches at us again."

However, the Spurs still had a few left, thanks to the combined 50-point, 30-rebound performances of Tim Duncan and Malik Rose as they won Game 5 in San Antonio, 94-82. San Antonio delivered the knockout punch of the series in Game 6, defeating the resilient Suns 87-85.

"I'm very proud of them," Suns coach Frank Johnson said. "I would have loved for us to go further, but we ran into a better team."

WESTERN CONFERENCE SEMIFINALS

GAME 1, *May 5, 2003*
San Antonio Spurs, 87
Los Angeles Lakers, 82

GAME 2, *May 7, 2003*
San Antonio Spurs, 114
Los Angeles Lakers, 95

GAME 3, *May 9, 2003*
Los Angeles Lakers, 110
San Antonio Spurs, 95

GAME 4, *May 11, 2003*
Los Angeles Lakers, 99
San Antonio Spurs, 95

GAME 5, *May 13, 2003*
San Antonio Spurs, 96
Los Angeles Lakers, 94

GAME 6, *May 15, 2003*
San Antonio Spurs, 110
Los Angeles Lakers, 82

This was the series the Spurs wanted. This was the series they needed. After the Los Angeles Lakers disposed of the Spurs in only nine games the last two postseasons, the Western Conference Semifinals would serve as the ultimate championship barometer for San Antonio. Was the team with the best regular-season record finally ready to knock off L.A.? Was the Spurs' sweep of the Lakers during the regular season a precursor of how the series will play out or was it merely a mirage? Is L.A., which stumbled during the first few months of the season, destined for a four-peat?

Unlike the previous two years, the Spurs struck first and provided some of the answers, winning Game 1, 87-82. Tim Duncan recorded an MVP type of performance with 28 points, eight rebounds and seven assists while rookie Manu Ginobili provided a spark off the bench, scoring 15 points.

"Tonight was a good stepping stone for us," Spurs forward Malik Rose said. "We just had a lot of guys step up and we just have to keep moving forward and build upon the success of this game."

In Game 2, the Spurs delivered another statement as they cruised to a 114-95 rout and at one point led by as many as 33 points. The Spurs received an offensive boost from forward Bruce Bowen who scored a career high 27 points, including a team playoff record seven three-pointers.

"It's the best game I've had as an NBA player," said Bowen. Despite the 2-0 series lead, the Spurs weren't doing any celebrating quite yet.

"They're the world champions," Parker said. "I don't think they respect us. I think, for them, this is nothing. We haven't beat them. To be up 2-0 is nothing."

Parker's words proved prophetic as San Antonio failed to capitalize on the momentum and blew a golden opportunity as they dropped the next two games in Los Angeles.

Suddenly, it was now a best two of three series as it shifted back to San Antonio. Would the Spurs respond or do the Lakers simply have their number in the postseason? The Spurs' answer appeared to be a resounding yes as they ran up a 25-point lead en route to what appeared to be an easy victory. However, blowing big leads has plagued the Spurs and this time was no different. The Lakers were within one point and with seconds remaining, got the ball in the hands of the man who has delivered so many times before for them — "Big Shot Rob" — Robert Horry. The anxious SBC crowd held its collective breath as Horry's three-pointer at the buzzer rattled in-and-out and the Spurs escaped with a breathtaking 96-94 win.

The Spurs didn't want to take any chances on a potential Game 7 matchup against the three-time defending NBA champions and closed the Lakers out on their home court in convincing fashion, routing them 110-82. Duncan once again dominated, collecting 37 points and 16 rebounds while Tony Parker came of age with a terrific 27-point performance. For L.A., dreams of a four-peat abruptly vanished while the Spurs finally unseated their playoff nemesis.

"We had a tough couple of years with these guys," said Spurs head coach Gregg Popovich. "To finally play well enough is beyond comprehension."

DALLAS

It was a Texas style show-down between two Midwest Division rivals featuring identical 60-22 records. After 82 regular-season games and two rounds of the playoffs under their belts, an NBA Finals appearance was now only four victories away. Don Nelson, the three-time NBA Coach of the Year winner, was making his first Western Conference Finals appearance as a head coach and after Game 1, was only three victories away from making his first in the Finals as well. Despite a 40-point, 15-rebound outburst by Tim Duncan, the Mavericks stunned the Spurs on their homecourt, winning 113-110. Dirk Nowitzki led the Mavs with 38 points, including a 17 for 17 performance from the line as Dallas converted a staggering 49 of their 50 free throw attempts. The Spurs bounced back in Game 2, thanks to Duncan's 32 points and 15 rebounds.

In Game 3, it was Tony Parker and not Duncan who took over the game. The 6-2 point guard scored 19 of his 29 points in the third quarter while

Duncan continued to pile on the numbers, recording 34 points, 24 rebounds, six assists and six blocks.

"[Parker] was great, hitting his shots, being aggressive in the open court," Duncan said. "Tony took it upon himself to push it up the court and make them pay."

The Mavs suffered a huge setback when Nowitzki collided with Manu Ginobili in the fourth quarter. The two-time NBA All-Star injured his left knee and was forced to leave the game. It would be his last appearance of the series.

The Mavericks "small ball" approach wasn't effective in Game 4 as Parker starred once again in the third quarter, scoring 11 of his 25 points, as the Spurs

WESTERN CONFERENCE FINALS

GAME 1, *May 19, 2003*
Dallas Mavericks, 113
San Antonio Spurs, 110

GAME 2, *May 21, 2003*
San Antonio Spurs, 119
Dallas Mavericks, 106

GAME 3, *May 23, 2003*
San Antonio Spurs, 96
Dallas Mavericks, 83

GAME 4, *May 25, 2003*
San Antonio Spurs, 102
Dallas Mavericks, 95

GAME 5, *May 27, 2003*
Dallas Mavericks, 103
San Antonio Spurs, 91

GAME 6, *May 29, 2003*
San Antonio Spurs, 90
Dallas Mavericks, 78

rolled to a 102-95 victory and a commanding 3-1 series lead.

With their first NBA Finals appearance in five years now within reach, the Spurs' plans for advancement were iced, courtesy of Michael Finley. The Dallas small forward scored 15 of his 31 points in the fourth quarter as the Mavs staved off elimination, winning Game 5, 103-91.

As the series shifted to Dallas, the momentum had shifted as well. The Spurs trailed by 13 points in the third quarter and a Game 7 showdown appeared likely. Starting point guard Tony Parker suffered from a stomach virus and was limited to 13 minutes of action while his backup, Speedy Claxton, was turning the ball over one too many times for head coach Gregg Popovich's liking. So Steve Kerr, the veteran guard who had played a total of 13 minutes in the postseason, including three in this series, was summoned from the Spurs' bench. Kerr quickly made his presence felt, nailing his first field goal attempt, a three-pointer from the corner with 1:38 remaining in the quarter. The three-point barrage continued early in the fourth ... *Manu Ginobili ...Boom!...Stephen Jackson ... Boom! ... Boom! ... Kerr ... Boom!* Suddenly, the game was tied at 71 apiece. Kerr wasn't finished. The 37-year-old sank two more treys as part of the Spurs amazing 23-0 run that resulted in a 90-78 victory and a Finals berth. For Kerr, the three-point flourish was all in a day's work. "I was wide open," said Kerr. "Those are shots I should hit."

NBA FINALS

BYRON SCOTT *New Jersey Nets head coach*

" *You have the best two teams in the league right here right now.* "

JULIUS ERVING *led the Nets to two ABA titles during his five-year ABA career.*

"To have us representing many members of the ABA, throughout history, it's a very humbling thing."

GAME ONE

IT WAS A REVOLUTIONARY LEAGUE THAT FEATURED SOME OF THE GAME'S GREATEST AND MOST INNOVATIVE PLAYERS. MORE THAN 25 YEARS HAVE PAST SINCE THE LAST ABA GAME WAS PLAYED YET THE UNMISTAKABLE RED, WHITE AND BLUE COLORS WERE ALIVE AND WELL AS TWO FORMER ABA LEGENDS TOOK PART IN THE CEREMONIAL OPENING TIP. WEARING THEIR ORIGINAL ABA JERSEYS, JULIUS ERVING AND GEORGE GERVIN, TWO OF THE LEAGUE'S BRIGHTEST STARS AND SHOWMEN, OFFICIALLY WELCOMED THIS HISTORIC OCCASION, MARKING THE FIRST TIME TWO FORMER ABA TEAMS HAVE MET IN THE NBA FINALS.

"PLAYING AGAINST THE BEST POINT GUARD IN THE LEAGUE MAKES ME WANT TO DO MORE AND PLAY MY BEST."

TONY PARKER

Game 1 of the 2003 NBA Finals marked the first time these two former rivals met in the postseason since the 1976 ABA Semifinals when Erving and the Nets defeated Gervin's Spurs in a thrilling seven-game series. Little did anyone know at the time that irony would play a small role in this rivalry coming full circle some 27 years later. Although the Spurs lost Game 7 to the Nets on April 24, 1976, the very next day, a gift from the basketball gods arrived in St. Croix. His name: Timothy Theodore Duncan.

Thanks to the two-time NBA MVP, Gervin and his former Spurs' teammates would get their revenge for at least one game. After a first half that saw both teams tied at 42 points apiece, the Spurs broke the game wide open in the third quarter, outscoring the Nets 32-17, which included a devastating 16-2 run. Demonstrating his brilliant all-around game, Duncan scored 13 points on 4-for-4 shooting while pulling down five rebounds and recording three assists and two steals in the quarter.

"The third quarter was a killer," said an emphatic Nets head coach, Byron Scott.

DUNCAN WASN'T THE LONE SPUR DOING THE DAMAGE. TONY PARKER, THE SECOND-YEAR POINT GUARD FROM FRANCE, ALSO LED THE WAY IN THE THIRD, SCORING NINE OF HIS 16 POINTS. THE NETS WERE REELING, STRUGGLING TO GENERATE SOME OFFENSE AS JASON KIDD CONNECTED ON ONLY 4 OF 17 SHOOTING FOR THE GAME, FINISHING WITH 10 POINTS.

"HE PLAYED A GREAT GAME. HE MADE SOME TOUGH SHOTS BUT HE'S DONE THAT FOR THEM FOR THE WHOLE SEASON, AND IN THE PLAYOFFS."

JASON KIDD *on Tony Parker*

"There's no excuse for me personally," said Kidd, who at one point missed 10 shots in a row. "I didn't shoot the ball extremely well. That's not what I'm known for."

The Spurs received an unexpected boost from an aggressive David Robinson, who turned back the clock and was an active force on both sides of the glass, swatting four shots, pulling down 6 rebounds and scoring 14 points.

"David was really important for us," said San Antonio head coach Gregg Popovich. "He realizes this is his last series, and I thought his effort defensively, board-wise, getting up and down the court was really superior, more than it has been in a while. He gave us everything his body will give us. It was really important to us."

The night, however, clearly belonged to Duncan, who recorded 32 points and 20 rebounds, marking only the eighth time in the last 20 years that a player has recorded 20-plus points and rebounds in a Finals game.

"I played him as tough as possible," said Kenyon Martin, who fouled out with 21 points. "I was riding him, tailing him. He just made tough shots. We executed our game plan when we had to. He just made tough shots."

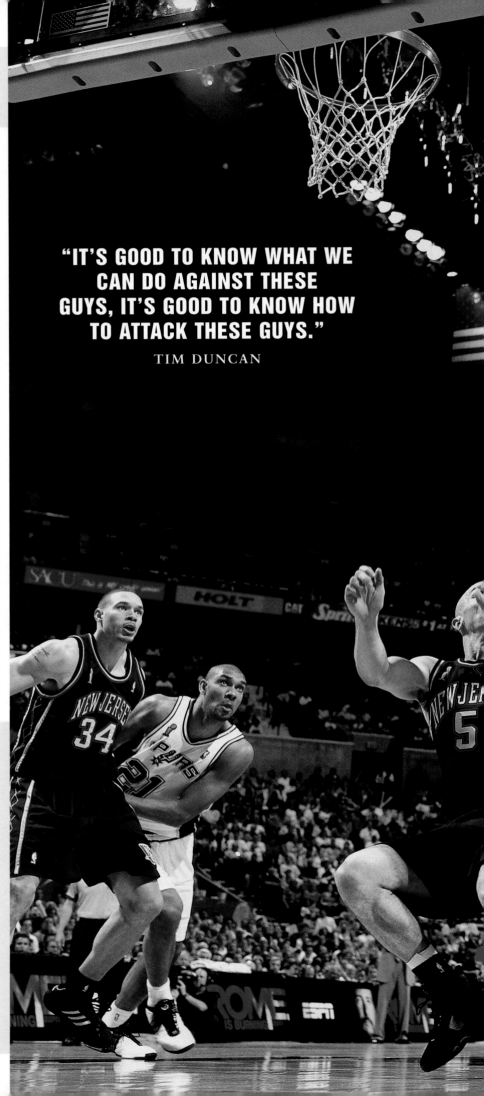

"IT'S GOOD TO KNOW WHAT WE CAN DO AGAINST THESE GUYS, IT'S GOOD TO KNOW HOW TO ATTACK THESE GUYS."

TIM DUNCAN

NEW JERSEY NETS

PLAYER	POS	MIN	FGM-A	3GM-A	FTM-A	OFF	DEF	TOT	AST	PF	ST	TO	BS	PTS
JASON KIDD	G	44	4-17	1-5	1-2	0	8	8	10	1	2	3	1	10
KERRY KITTLES	G	30	2-7	1-3	3-4	2	1	3	2	1	0	1	0	8
RICHARD JEFFERSON	F	36	5-10	0-0	5-6	0	4	4	1	3	2	3	0	15
KENYON MARTIN	F	33	10-24	0-1	1-2	4	8	12	2	6	1	1	2	21
JASON COLLINS	C	31	1-4	0-0	3-4	4	5	9	3	4	0	0	0	5
Lucious Harris		24	4-10	1-2	6-7	0	1	1	0	1	0	0	0	15
Rodney Rogers		21	5-10	1-2	0-0	1	1	2	1	3	0	0	0	11
Aaron Williams		11	2-5	0-0	0-0	2	2	4	0	4	0	0	1	4
Dikembe Mutombo		6	0-1	0-0	0-0	0	2	2	0	2	0	0	1	0
Anthony Johnson		4	0-1	0-0	0-0	0	0	0	0	1	0	0	0	0
Tamar Slay	+	DNP	+	+	+	+	+	+	+	+	+	+	+	+
Brian Scalabrine	+	DNP	+	+	+	+	+	+	+	+	+	+	+	+
TOTAL		240	33-89	4-13	19-25	13	32	45	19	26	5	8	5	89
			(37.1)	(30.8)	(76.0)	Team Rebs: 11								

SAN ANTONIO SPURS

PLAYER	POS	MIN	FGM-A	3GM-A	FTM-A	OFF	DEF	TOT	AST	PF	ST	TO	BS	PTS
STEPHEN JACKSON	G	42	5-15	0-4	2-5	1	2	3	5	3	2	3	0	12
TONY PARKER	G	40	6-14	1-2	3-4	0	3	3	5	0	1	2	0	16
TIM DUNCAN	F	44	11-17	0-0	10-14	3	17	20	6	1	3	1	7	32
BRUCE BOWEN	F	26	2-3	2-2	0-0	0	2	2	1	4	0	1	0	6
DAVID ROBINSON	C	27	6-8	0-0	2-3	2	4	6	1	2	0	0	4	14
Emanuel Ginobili		28	3-8	1-2	0-0	1	6	7	3	3	0	3	0	7
Malik Rose		24	5-11	0-0	2-2	3	3	6	2	5	1	2	0	12
Speedy Claxton		8	1-3	0-0	0-0	0	0	0	1	2	0	0	1	2
Danny Ferry		1	0-0	0-0	0-0	0	0	0	0	0	0	0	0	0
Steve Kerr	+	DNP	+	+	+	+	+	+	+	+	+	+	+	+
Steve Smith	+	DNP	+	+	+	+	+	+	+	+	+	+	+	+
Kevin Willis	+	DNP	+	+	+	+	+	+	+	+	+	+	+	+
TOTAL		240	39-79	4-10	19-28	10	37	47	24	20	7	12	12	101
			(49.4)	(40.0)	(67.9)	Team Rebs: 8								

DIKEMBE MUTOMBO

"For some reason, I've been praying more than I have done in my life. I haven't seen so many things happen in my life as have happened to me this year."

GAME TWO

HE WAS THE NETS FORGOTTEN MAN. A FOUR-TIME NBA DEFENSIVE PLAYER OF THE YEAR WHO LANGUISHED ON THE BENCH AFTER TEARING LIGAMENTS IN HIS WRIST WHILE MISSING 56 REGULAR-SEASON GAMES. A PROUD MAN WHO FELT THE PAIN OF LOSING HIS 40-YEAR-OLD BROTHER TO AN UNEXPECTED DEATH RIGHT BEFORE THE PLAYOFFS. A MAN WHO FINALLY HEALED PHYSI-CALLY BUT STILL WAS ON THE OUTSIDE LOOKING IN WHEN IT CAME TO PLAYING TIME AS HE WATCHED HIS TEAM RIDE A 10-GAME WINNING STREAK ALL THE WAY TO THE NBA FINALS. THIS CERTAINLY WASN'T THE SEASON DIKEMBE MUTOMBO HAD ENVISIONED WHEN THE NETS ACQUIRED HIM ON AUGUST 6, 2002.

"IT CHANGES THE WHOLE OUTLOOK OF OUR DEFENSE. NOW THEY HAVE TO CONTEND WITH MOUNT MUTOMBO."

JASON KIDD

"**I** was told I was brought here to help the organization win the championship," Mutombo said. "And here we are in the championship, and I'm sitting on the bench."

Despite the disappointment, Mutombo didn't lose faith or focus on the Nets championship mission. When head coach Byron Scott called his number in the second quarter, the center who played a productive six minutes in Game 1, provided New Jersey with a huge lift and was instrumental in securing the franchise's first-ever NBA Finals victory.

Mutombo was inserted into the second quarter and immediately made his presence felt as the Nets outscored the Spurs 22-17 to take the half-time lead. The tireless center scored two quick baskets to give New Jersey the lead and was a defensive menace, limiting San Antonio's penetration and second shot attempts as the Spurs shot just 6 for 18 in the quarter. Most importantly, Mutombo, who also saw action in the fourth quarter, helped slow down the NBA's MVP Tim Duncan, who dominated the first game with a 32-point, 20-rebound performance. Duncan was limited to 19 points and 12 rebounds.

"HE PLAYED GREAT TONIGHT," SAID NETS FORWARD KENYON MARTIN, WHO SCORED 14 POINTS. "DEKE GAVE US ENERGY, HE GAVE US A COUPLE OF BASKETS, A COUPLE OF BLOCKS. HE GAVE US A LOT OF SIZE."

"I THINK THAT WE SHOWED A REAL LACK OF RESPECT FOR THE SITUATION THROUGH THREE QUARTERS. WHEN IT FINALLY GOT CRITICAL, IT LOOKED LIKE THE BASKETBALL TEAM THAT I'VE WATCHED PLAY ALL YEAR LONG. BUT YOU CAN'T PLAY LIKE THAT IN AN NBA FINALS GAME."

GREGG POPOVICH *San Antonio Spurs head coach*

What Mutombo was to the Nets defensively, Jason Kidd was offensively. The All-Star point guard shook a 4 for 17 shooting slump in Game 1 and scored 30 points, including the last seven for New Jersey.

"He was on attack mode all night long," said Nets head coach Byron Scott. "He did a heck of a job of being offensively aggressive."

The Spurs didn't help their cause by turning the ball over 21 times while also missing 14 of 25 free throws.

"When we do that, we put a lot of pressure on our defense," said Spurs head coach Gregg Popovich. "Those two areas cropped up and that was the ballgame."

Duncan, in particular, had an off night by his standards and struggled from the free throw line, connecting on only 3 for 10 attempts.

'When it came down to it, I missed seven free throws," said Duncan, who missed three in the final 3:39 of regulation. "I make a couple of those, it's a whole different ballgame."

The Spurs did make a valiant comeback and had a chance to go up 2-0 in the series but Stephen Jackson's three-pointer rimmed out at the buzzer and the Nets headed home to East Rutherford, N.J., with the Finals tied one game apiece.

For Mutombo, it was his most important game of this season and it couldn't have come at a better time.

"I'm not trying to dominate and try to push nobody away," said Mutombo in reference to Jason Collins and Aaron Williams. "I just want to feel like I'm part of this group."

"JASON IS THE BACKBONE OF THIS TEAM AND TONIGHT WE DID A MUCH BETTER JOB OF FEEDING OFF HIS ENERGY."

RICHARD JEFFERSON

NEW JERSEY NETS

PLAYER	POS	MIN	FGM-A	3GM-A	FTM-A	OFF	DEF	TOT	AST	PF	ST	TO	BS	PTS
						REBOUNDS								
JASON KIDD	G	42	11-24	2-4	6-8	4	3	7	3	1	0	4	0	30
KERRY KITTLES	G	21	3-7	1-2	1-2	1	3	4	1	1	3	1	0	8
RICHARD JEFFERSON	F	39	3-10	0-0	2-2	1	2	3	3	3	2	3	0	8
KENYON MARTIN	F	33	6-16	0-0	2-2	3	2	5	4	5	2	1	2	14
JASON COLLINS	C	34	3-6	0-1	0-0	1	3	4	1	2	1	1	0	6
Lucious Harris		27	5-8	0-1	0-0	2	5	7	1	1	1	1	0	10
Dikembe Mutombo		20	2-3	0-0	0-0	1	3	4	0	3	0	0	3	4
Rodney Rogers		18	2-8	1-3	2-2	2	3	5	2	4	0	1	0	7
Anthony Johnson		6	0-1	0-0	0-0	0	0	0	1	1	0	1	0	0
Tamar Slay	+	DNP	+	+	+	+	+	+	+	+	+	+	+	+
Aaron Williams	+	DNP	+	+	+	+	+	+	+	+	+	+	+	+
Brian Scalabrine	+	DNP	+	+	+	+	+	+	+	+	+	+	+	+
TOTAL		240	35-83	4-11	13-16	15	24	39	16	21	9	13	5	87
			(42.2)	(36.4)	(81.3)	Team Rebs: 5								

SAN ANTONIO SPURS

PLAYER	POS	MIN	FGM-A	3GM-A	FTM-A	OFF	DEF	TOT	AST	PF	ST	TO	BS	PTS
						REBOUNDS								
TONY PARKER	G	41	9-17	0-2	3-4	1	4	5	5	3	0	1	1	21
STEPHEN JACKSON	G	40	6-10	4-7	0-0	0	2	2	3	2	2	7	1	16
TIM DUNCAN	F	43	8-19	0-1	3-10	2	10	12	3	3	0	4	3	19
BRUCE BOWEN	F	26	1-2	1-1	0-0	0	5	5	0	1	0	2	0	3
DAVID ROBINSON	C	33	3-6	0-0	4-6	4	4	8	1	0	2	1	2	10
Emanuel Ginobili		29	1-6	0-2	2-2	4	2	6	3	4	1	3	0	4
Malik Rose		19	3-4	0-0	1-1	2	1	3	1	1	1	2	0	7
Speedy Claxton		7	2-2	0-0	1-2	0	0	0	0	0	0	1	0	5
Steve Kerr		1	0-1	0-0	0-0	0	0	0	1	2	0	0	0	0
Kevin Willis		1	0-1	0-0	0-0	1	1	2	0	0	0	0	0	0
Danny Ferry	+	DNP	+	+	+	+	+	+	+	+	+	+	+	+
Steve Smith	+	DNP	+	+	+	+	+	+	+	+	+	+	+	+
TOTAL		240	33-68	5-13	14-25	14	29	43	17	16	6	21	7	85
			(48.5)	(38.5)	(56.0)	Team Rebs: 10								

GREGG POPOVICH *on his young Spurs' players*

"It's fun for them and it's a life-shortening experience for me. I'm being honest. I think I have about a week left."

GAME THREE

TONY PARKER REMEMBERS IT CLEARLY. SAME WITH MANU GINOBILI. EVEN THOUGH THE TWO SAN ANTONIO SPURS' TEAMMATES GREW UP IN DIFFERENT PARTS OF THE WORLD, THE IMPACT OF WATCHING THEIR FIRST NBA FINALS AS YOUNGSTERS WAS THE SAME LIFE-CHANGING EXPERIENCE.

"I SAW MICHAEL JORDAN ON TV IN THE FINALS, AND I KNEW I WANTED TO PLAY BASKETBALL," SAID PARKER, WHO WAS BORN IN BRUGES, BELGIUM AND WAS RAISED IN FRANCE.

SAID GINOBILI, WHO WAS BORN IN ARGENTINA: "I WAS CRAZY FOR IT. ALL OF M.J.'S SHOTS, THOSE BIG SHOTS, STEVE KERR, JOHN PAXSON. I WAS CRAZY FOR THAT TEAM."

SO THERE IS LITTLE DOUBT THAT WITH MORE THAN 3.1 BILLION PEOPLE TUNING IN TO THIS YEAR'S NBA FINALS FROM 205 COUNTRIES ALL OVER THE WORLD THAT SOME ASPIRING BASKETBALL PLAYER WASN'T EQUALLY AS MOVED IN WATCHING PARKER AND GINOBILI PERFORM IN THEIR NEW ROLES AS NBA FINALS HEROES.

The Spurs international backcourt was instrumental in San Antonio's 84-79 victory over the Nets, bringing the Spurs one step closer to their second NBA title in five years. After both teams tied an NBA record for the low-est combined half-time score in NBA Finals history with 63 points, Parker, the 6-2 point guard, heated up in the second half. The second-year player scored 19 points, including four three-pointers and outscored Jason Kidd, the Nets All-Star point guard, 26-12.

"I TRY NOT TO PUT TOO MUCH PRESSURE ON MYSELF," SAID PARKER, WHO ALSO OUTSCORED KIDD 10-2 IN THE FOURTH QUARTER. "THE MAIN THING IS, IT'S THE SPURS AGAINST THE NEW JERSEY NETS. I JUST TRY TO RUN MY TEAM AND TRY TO BE AGGRESSIVE. COACH POP WANTS ME TO BE AGGRESSIVE AND THAT'S WHAT I'M TRYING TO DO."

When he wasn't raining threes, Parker was penetrating the lane at will, lofting floaters over the outstretched Net defenders.

"Tony is a special young man," said Spurs head coach Gregg Popovich. "To be thrown into that situation as young as he is, to try to run the club, know all the players — to handle all that I think is special. I am really impressed at what he can do at a young age."

Ginobili came up huge for the Spurs in the second half, scoring all eight of his points and coming up with a few clutch plays in the game's closing

"TONY IS A SPECIAL YOUNG MAN. TO BE THROWN INTO THAT SITUATION AS YOUNG AS HE IS, TO TRY TO RUN THE CLUB, KNOW ALL THE PLAYERS — TO HANDLE ALL THAT I THINK IS SPECIAL."

GREGG POPOVICH *San Antonio Spurs head coach*

"IT'S NOT A MAJOR SETBACK. THEY DID WHAT WE HAD DONE LAST GAME. THEY TOOK BACK HOMECOURT."

BYRON SCOTT *New Jersey Nets head coach*

moments. With 1:18 remaining and the Nets trailing 78-75, Ginobili stole the ball from Nets guard Lucious Harris, which eventually led to two Parker free throws. When the point guard missed his second consecutive attempt, Tim Duncan skillfully outmaneuvered Kenyon Martin, slipping behind him to grab a crucial rebound. Duncan found Parker who then fed Ginobili who hit a baseline floater with 43.2 seconds left. The basket gave the Spurs a five-point cushion.

"I don't think they expected a shot from me," said Ginobili following the victory. "It's not always Tim and Tony. Someone else can get lucky once in awhile."

The Spurs 3-2 zone defense in the second and fourth quarters was key in shutting down the fastbreaking Nets who turned the ball over 18 times and shot just 37 percent from the field. Parker and Bowen were particularly effective on Kidd and Richard Jefferson, who struggled, scoring six points on 3 for 11 shooting. The Spurs also prevented New Jersey from making a field goal during a six-minute stretch in the fourth quarter.

"IT'S FRUSTRATING TO A CERTAIN EXTENT," SAID NETS GUARD KERRY KITTLES WHO SCORED 21 POINTS. "WE WERE TRYING TO MOVE THE BALL AGAINST THEIR ZONE, BUT THEY DID A GOOD JOB OF MATCHING UP AGAINST US AND CONTESTING JUMP SHOTS. THEN, IF YOU PUT THE BALL ON THE FLOOR AND TRY TO DRIVE IN THE PAINT, YOU HAVE A TOUGH SHOT OVER THEIR 7-FOOTERS."

"THAT DUNK CAME AS A BIG SURPRISE. IT WAS ONE OF THOSE THINGS WHERE YOU ALMOST HAVE TO ASK YOURSELF: 'DID THAT JUST HAPPEN?' WE WERE ALL JUST STUNNED."

RODNEY ROGERS *on Malik Rose's fourth-quarter dunk that started a 14-3 San Antonio run*

SAN ANTONIO SPURS

PLAYER	POS	MIN	FGM-A	3GM-A	FTM-A	OFF	DEF	TOT	AST	PF	ST	TO	BS	PTS
TONY PARKER	G	43	9-21	4-6	4-8	1	2	3	6	0	0	1	0	26
STEPHEN JACKSON	G	36	2-7	1-2	2-4	0	6	6	2	3	1	4	0	7
TIM DUNCAN	F	45	6-13	0-0	9-12	3	13	16	7	3	1	5	3	21
BRUCE BOWEN	F	32	0-5	0-2	0-0	1	3	4	0	3	1	1	2	0
DAVID ROBINSON	C	26	1-5	0-0	6-8	1	2	3	0	2	1	0	0	8
Emanuel Ginobili		28	3-6	0-0	2-3	2	0	2	4	2	4	1	2	8
Malik Rose		22	4-7	0-0	0-0	0	2	2	0	2	1	3	1	8
Speedy Claxton		5	2-2	0-0	0-0	0	1	1	0	1	1	1	0	4
Kevin Willis		3	1-1	0-0	0-0	1	0	1	0	1	0	1	0	2
Steve Kerr	+	DNP	+	+	+	+	+	+	+	+	+	+	+	+
Danny Ferry	+	DNP	+	+	+	+	+	+	+	+	+	+	+	+
Steve Smith	+	DNP	+	+	+	+	+	+	+	+	+	+	+	+
TOTAL		240	28-67	5-10	23-35	9	29	38	19	17	10	17	8	84

(41.8) (50.0) (65.7)   Team Rebs: 15

NEW JERSEY NETS

PLAYER	POS	MIN	FGM-A	3GM-A	FTM-A	OFF	DEF	TOT	AST	PF	ST	TO	BS	PTS
JASON KIDD	G	42	6-19	0-5	0-0	2	1	3	11	3	2	4	0	12
KERRY KITTLES	G	34	8-16	3-5	2-3	1	3	4	1	2	3	0	2	21
KENYON MARTIN	F	42	8-18	0-1	7-8	2	9	11	0	5	4	5	2	23
RICHARD JEFFERSON	F	36	3-11	0-0	0-0	2	7	9	0	2	2	1	0	6
JASON COLLINS	C	25	0-3	0-0	0-0	4	1	5	1	6	0	3	1	0
Lucious Harris		22	1-6	1-2	4-4	1	0	1	3	2	1	2	0	7
Dikembe Mutombo		18	1-1	0-0	0-0	1	2	3	0	3	1	1	0	2
Rodney Rogers		11	0-3	0-0	2-2	0	2	2	0	2	0	2	0	2
Anthony Johnson		6	2-2	0-0	0-0	0	1	1	0	0	0	0	0	4
Aaron Williams		4	1-2	0-0	0-0	1	1	2	1	1	0	0	0	2
Tamar Slay	+	DNP	+	+	+	+	+	+	+	+	+	+	+	+
Brian Scalabrine	+	DNP	+	+	+	+	+	+	+	+	+	+	+	+
TOTAL		240	30-81	4-13	15-17	14	27	41	17	26	13	18	5	79

(37.0) (30.8) (88.2)   Team Rebs: 10

JEWEL

GEORGE STRAIT

TOMMY LEE JONES

TIM ROBBINS

KELLY ROWLAND

ALL ACCESS

MARTIE MAGUIRE & NATALIE MAINES OF THE DIXIE CHICKS

JOUMANA AND T.J. KIDD WITH BRUCE WILLIS

BYRON SCOTT

"RJ came to life."

GAME FOUR

THE NEW JERSEY NETS WERE ON THE ROPES. AN AIR OF HOPE AND DESPERA-TION FLUTTERED AROUND CONTINENTAL AIRLINES ARENA HOURS BEFORE TIPOFF AS THE EASTERN CONFERENCE CHAMPIONS, WHO FACED A 2-1 SERIES DEFICIT, COULDN'T AFFORD TO LOSE A PIVOTAL GAME 4. AFTER ALL, NO TEAM IN NBA FINALS HISTORY HAS EVER COME BACK FROM A 3-1 SERIES DEFICIT TO WIN THE CHAMPIONSHIP.

"WE HAD TO TREAT GAME 4 LIKE IT WAS GAME 7," SAID NETS FORWARD KENYON MARTIN. "THE ODDS ON 3-1 AIN'T THAT GREAT; 2-2 IS A LOT BETTER."

THE PRESSURE CLEARLY MOUNTED FOR THE EASTERN CONFERENCE CHAMPIONS BUT NO PLAYER FELT THE BURDEN OF GREAT EXPECTATIONS MORE SO THAN THEIR SMALL FORWARD, RICHARD JEFFERSON. NICKNAMED "YOUNG FELLA" BY HIS TEAMMATES, JEFFERSON LABORED THROUGH THE FIRST THREE GAMES OF THE SERIES, AVERAGING 9.7 POINTS, NEARLY SIX LESS THAN HIS REGULAR-SEASON AVERAGE. IN THE TWO PREVIOUS GAMES, THE 22-YEAR-OLD SCORED A COMBINED 14 POINTS ON 6-FOR-21 SHOOTING.

"HE HAS NOT HAD A GOOD GAME YET," SAID NETS POINT GUARD JASON KIDD, "SO WE JUST NEED HIM TO RELAX, GO OUT THERE, BE R.J., AND LET THE GAME COME TO HIM."

Jefferson did just that in the first half, slashing and driving his way to 10 points and eight rebounds as the Nets stormed to a 14-2 run with 3:32 remaining in the second quarter while Tim Duncan sat on the San Antonio bench with three fouls.

In the third quarter, Jefferson punctuated his comeback game with an "RJ Special," a one-handed windmill baseline dunk over the Spurs' Kevin Willis that rocked the 19,280 fans in attendance.

"That was one of those amazing RJ plays," said Nets forward Aaron Williams. "We've been waiting all series to see one of those. He brought it out and it was nice."

Ironically, the momentum quickly dissipated for Jefferson and the Nets. The second-year player missed his next four shots while the team also struggled, missing its final 10 attempts of the quarter. Suddenly, the Nets' 15-point lead evaporated as San Antonio outscored New Jersey 23-11 in the third quarter, thanks to the inspired play of Spurs' reserve point guard Speedy Claxton and the rebounding efforts of Duncan, who limited plenty of second-chance shot opportunities.

With the Nets trailing 72-71 with 1:15 remaining and their season clearly on the brink, Kenyon Martin's determined efforts under the basket in one sequence typified his team's desire to extend the series. In a flurry of activity, Martin powered his way up to the basket only to have his field goal attempt blocked not once but twice by Duncan on successive occasions. The Nets' emotional leader persevered and grabbed both offensive rebounds and went up a third time only to be fouled by Kevin Willis, sending him to the free throw line.

"I wasn't satisfied when he blocked the first one and [I] got it back and [he] blocked the second one," said Martin of Duncan. "I was in that mode all game, in attack mode, getting to the rim and I did a decent job of it."

Trailing by one point, the Spurs had their chance to reclaim the lead after a pair of Jason Kidd jumpers missed but on each occasion the ball fell into the hands of the opportunistic Nets.

"We just lost the offensive rebound to put ourselves in the toughest position, and then you give the second one away, you just feel like kicking yourself," said David Robinson, who fouled out of the game.

TRAILING 77-74, THE SPURS DID HAVE ONE LAST CHANCE TO TIE THE GAME BUT GINOBILI'S THREE-POINTER WITH 2.7 SECONDS LEFT MISSED AS DUNCAN SCOOPED UP THE REBOUND AND SCORED ON THE FOLLOW UP AS THE BUZZER SOUNDED.

The Nets prevailed, winning by one point and climbed back into the series while the Spurs bemoaned their missed opportunity to go up 3-1. The Spurs shot only 28.9 percent from the field.

"The next game, I guarantee those guys won't shoot like that," said Duncan, who collected 23 points and 17 rebounds. "I guarantee those guys will make shots. Things will be different."

"I UNDERSTAND THAT IN ORDER FOR THIS TEAM TO BE SUCCESSFUL AND WIN A CHAMPIONSHIP, I HAVE TO PLAY WELL."

RICHARD JEFFERSON

SAN ANTONIO SPURS

PLAYER	POS	MIN	FGM-A	3GM-A	FTM-A	REBOUNDS OFF	DEF	TOT	AST	PF	ST	TO	BS	PTS
TONY PARKER	G	31	1-12	0-2	1-2	0	4	4	3	3	0	2	0	3
STEPHEN JACKSON	G	28	1-9	1-4	2-3	2	2	4	3	3	1	2	1	5
BRUCE BOWEN	F	40	2-9	1-5	0-0	1	6	7	1	2	2	0	0	5
TIM DUNCAN	F	39	10-23	0-0	3-3	8	9	17	2	4	1	3	7	23
DAVID ROBINSON	C	24	4-5	0-0	6-7	3	4	7	1	6	1	0	1	14
Emanuel Ginobili		28	3-10	2-6	2-3	1	1	2	1	1	4	1	0	10
Speedy Claxton		17	3-6	0-0	4-4	1	2	3	2	1	1	0	0	10
Kevin Willis		16	2-7	0-0	2-2	5	0	5	0	3	0	2	1	6
Malik Rose		15	0-9	0-1	0-0	1	3	4	0	3	0	1	0	0
Steve Kerr		1	0-0	0-0	0-0	0	0	0	1	1	0	0	0	0
Danny Ferry		1	0-0	0-0	0-0	0	0	0	0	0	0	0	0	0
Steve Smith	+	DNP	+	+	+	+	+	+	+	+	+	+	+	+
TOTAL		240	26-90	4-18	20-24	22	31	53	14	27	10	11	10	76
			(28.9)	(22.2)	(83.3)	Team Rebs: 12								

NEW JERSEY NETS

PLAYER	POS	MIN	FGM-A	3GM-A	FTM-A	REBOUNDS OFF	DEF	TOT	AST	PF	ST	TO	BS	PTS
JASON KIDD	G	47	5-18	0-4	6-6	3	5	8	9	3	0	5	0	16
KERRY KITTLES	G	35	2-10	0-4	0-0	1	5	6	1	0	1	0	0	4
KENYON MARTIN	F	40	7-16	0-0	6-12	5	8	13	3	5	1	5	3	20
RICHARD JEFFERSON	F	40	8-15	0-0	2-4	1	9	10	1	1	0	3	2	18
JASON COLLINS	C	10	0-0	0-0	0-0	2	0	2	1	4	1	0	1	0
Dikembe Mutombo		21	1-3	0-0	2-2	2	1	3	0	3	2	1	3	4
Aaron Williams		17	2-6	0-0	4-5	2	5	7	1	3	0	0	4	8
Lucious Harris		15	0-4	0-0	0-0	3	1	4	3	1	0	1	0	0
Rodney Rogers		11	2-5	0-0	0-0	0	0	0	0	2	0	1	0	4
Anthony Johnson		4	1-1	1-1	0-0	0	0	0	0	0	0	0	0	3
Tamar Slay	+	DNP	+	+	+	+	+	+	+	+	+	+	+	+
Brian Scalabrine	+	DNP	+	+	+	+	+	+	+	+	+	+	+	+
TOTAL		240	28-78	1-9	20-29	19	34	53	19	22	5	16	13	77
			(35.9)	(11.1)	(69.0)	Team Rebs: 9								

STEVE KERR

"I've got the greatest job on earth. I play six minutes, hit a few shots and come in and do interviews. It's awesome."

GAME FIVE

THE NICKNAME DOESN'T APPEAR ON T-SHIRTS OR HATS NOR WILL IT BE FEATURED IN COMMERCIALS ANY TIME SOON. IT IS A NAME THAT WAS BORN FROM LAST-SECOND HEROICS DURING GAME 6 OF THE 1997 NBA FINALS AS A MEMBER OF THE CHICAGO BULLS AND CONTINUES TO BLOSSOM SOME SIX YEARS LATER. STEVE KERR LOVES PLAYING THE ROLE OF BASKETBALL SAVIOR FOR THE SAN ANTONIO SPURS. IT IS A ROLE THAT SUITS HIM WELL, EVIDENCED BY HIS GAME 6 THREE-POINT SHOOTING DISPLAY AGAINST THE DALLAS MAVERICKS IN THE WESTERN CONFERENCE FINALS WHEN HE LED THE SPURS TO THEIR IMPROBABLE COMEBACK VICTORY. MR. FOURTH QUARTER WAS CALLED UPON ONCE AGAIN, THIS TIME WITH 9:02 REMAINING IN THE GAME WITH THE SPURS CLINGING TO A 70-65 LEAD.

Kerr, who only played a combined two minutes in the first four games of the series, made his presence felt on the defensive end with 3:21 remaining as the Nets, trailing by two, looked to tie the game. Operating within a 3-2 zone defense, Kerr alertly reached in with his left hand and stripped the ball from Nets forward Kenyon Martin. Kerr then wisely fired a pass down court, which led to a Spurs timeout.

"I knew that Kenyon loves that fake to the baseline and middle penetration," Kerr said. "He loves going middle, and so I just anticipated it and got my hand on the ball."

The play set the stage for even more Kerr heroics. As the Nets double teamed Spurs forward Tim Duncan, an open Kerr patiently waited outside the three-point line for the pass and, *boom!*, just like that, the Spurs led 83-76.

Mr. Fourth Quarter then followed up with a 15-foot jumper with 1:41 remaining in the game, giving the Spurs an 87-78 lead.

"Steve saved the day again," said Spurs guard Stephen Jackson. "He just stays ready."

Duncan, who overwhelmed the Nets with 29 points, 17 rebounds and 4 blocks, sees Kerr as a double-team savior.

"I love to get the ball on the post and see a guy trying to step off him a little bit and to throw that ball out to him," said Duncan. "Every time I throw it out to

"I HAVE THE EXPERIENCE TO NOT GET NERVOUS. I'VE DONE THIS A LOT."

STEVE KERR

him I hope he shoots it, because I really do believe it's going in every time."

Jason Kidd led the Nets in scoring with 29 points but New Jersey missed the usual 20-point, 9-rebound averages by Martin. The third-year forward was suffering from the flu and his game suffered as a result, scoring only four points and committing eight turnovers.

"It was just a bad game at the wrong time," said a dejected Martin.

KERR WASN'T THE ONLY SPURS' RESERVE TO RESPOND IN THIS CRUCIAL GAME. MALIK ROSE SCORED 14 POINTS ON 6-FOR-9 SHOOTING, WHICH SERVED AS A BOUNCE-BACK PERFORMANCE FOR THE FORWARD WHO WENT SCORE-LESS IN THE PREVIOUS GAME.

"After Game 4, I was just really frustrated, angry with myself," said Rose. "I felt like I let my team down. I was just looking forward to coming out. I didn't know how many shots I was going to make, I was just going to take them all confidently and play aggressively and things worked out well."

After the game, Kerr was basking in the attention as he reflected on his past play-off glories.

"I've been there many times and I've gotten over that nervousness," said Kerr, the NBA's all-time leader in three-point percentage. "I'm at a point in my career now where I just understand -- just shoot if you're open. If you miss, you miss, but you just let it fly."

"I'D RATHER BE WHERE WE ARE THAN WHERE THEY ARE."
TIM DUNCAN

"IT'S NOT IMPOSSIBLE, THE SITUATION THAT WE'RE IN. NOW, WHEN YOU TALK ABOUT 'MUST-WINS,' THIS IS A 'MUST-WIN.'"
BYRON SCOTT *referring to Game 6*

SAN ANTONIO SPURS

PLAYER	POS	MIN	FGM-A	3GM-A	FTM-A	OFF	DEF	TOT	AST	PF	ST	TO	BS	PTS
TONY PARKER	G	33	5-13	1-2	3-5	0	2	2	4	3	1	2	0	14
STEPHEN JACKSON	G	32	2-7	1-4	0-0	1	6	7	3	2	0	4	0	5
TIM DUNCAN	F	46	10-18	0-0	9-10	3	14	17	4	3	1	6	4	29
BRUCE BOWEN	F	29	1-4	0-2	2-2	0	1	1	1	4	0	0	0	4
DAVID ROBINSON	C	20	2-4	0-0	2-2	1	2	3	0	6	3	1	2	6
Malik Rose		29	6-9	0-0	2-2	2	1	3	1	2	0	1	0	14
Emanuel Ginobili		26	4-8	0-0	4-4	0	3	3	0	5	2	1	1	12
Speedy Claxton		15	1-4	0-0	1-2	0	1	1	2	4	2	0	2	3
Steve Kerr		9	2-2	1-1	1-2	1	0	1	0	0	1	0	0	6
Kevin Willis		1	0-0	0-0	0-0	0	1	1	0	0	0	0	0	0
Danny Ferry	+	DNP	+	+	+	+	+	+	+	+	+	+	+	+
Steve Smith	+	DNP	+	+	+	+	+	+	+	+	+	+	+	+
TOTAL		240	33-69	3-9	24-29	8	31	39	15	29	10	15	9	93
			(47.8)	(33.3)	(82.8)				Team Rebs: 8					

NEW JERSEY NETS

PLAYER	POS	MIN	FGM-A	3GM-A	FTM-A	OFF	DEF	TOT	AST	PF	ST	TO	BS	PTS
JASON KIDD	G	48	10-23	4-10	5-6	3	4	7	7	2	2	2	0	29
KERRY KITTLES	G	34	3-9	0-3	2-2	1	3	4	1	3	1	1	1	8
KENYON MARTIN	F	38	2-8	0-1	0-0	1	8	9	3	5	1	8	3	4
RICHARD JEFFERSON	F	37	5-11	0-0	9-11	2	4	6	4	4	2	1	0	19
JASON COLLINS	C	26	1-3	0-0	5-6	4	1	5	0	5	1	0	0	7
Aaron Williams		23	4-9	0-0	2-3	4	3	7	0	4	0	0	1	10
Lucious Harris		22	1-7	0-0	3-4	0	1	1	0	0	0	1	0	5
Dikembe Mutombo		7	0-1	0-0	0-0	1	1	2	0	2	0	2	0	0
Rodney Rogers		5	0-3	0-2	1-2	1	0	1	0	0	0	1	0	1
Tamar Slay	+	DNP	+	+	+	+	+	+	+	+	+	+	+	+
Anthony Johnson	+	DNP	+	+	+	+	+	+	+	+	+	+	+	+
Brian Scalabrine	+	DNP	+	+	+	+	+	+	+	+	+	+	+	+
TOTAL		240	26-74	4-16	27-34	17	25	42	15	25	7	16	5	83
			(35.1)	(25.0)	(79.4)				Team Rebs: 7					

GREGG POPOVICH

"I'm just thrilled that David ended his career with a game like that. His effort was really wonderful. He really dug down deep and showed how important it was to him to help us get this victory."

GAME SIX

THE ENDING WAS STORYBOOK, AN EXCLAMATION POINT ON A BRILLIANT CAREER AND ONE ALL ATHLETES DREAM ABOUT WHEN THAT INEVITABLE DAY ARRIVES. DAVID ROBINSON PLAYED 14 SEASONS, SCORED MORE THAN 20,000 POINTS AND GRABBED MORE THAN 10,000 REBOUNDS AND WITH 35.6 SECONDS REMAINING RECEIVED THE ULTIMATE CHAMPIONSHIP CURTAIN CALL. ROBINSON EXHALED, WALKING OFF THE COURT FOR ONE LAST TIME TO THE SPURS BENCH AS AN ADOR-ING SOLD-OUT SBC CROWD SALUTED THEIR FAVORITE ADMIRAL THE ONLY WAY THEY KNEW HOW, WITH A THUNDEROUS OVATION.

IT WAS A GLORIOUS MOMENT, ONE THAT WAS FITTING OF A CHAMPION. IT WAS ALSO A MOMENT OF FINALITY AS ROBINSON'S TEAMMATES SAID GOODBYE FOR ONE LAST TIME.

"THE LAST COUPLE OF SECONDS I REALLY THOUGHT, 'YOU KNOW WHAT, I'M NOT GOING TO PLAY WITH THIS GUY AGAIN,'" SAID TIM DUNCAN. "I'M GOING TO HAVE TO COME OUT ON THIS COURT WITHOUT HIM. IT'S GOING TO BE WEIRD."

For 39 minutes, the championship celebration was in doubt as the New Jersey Nets were doing their best to host a victory party of their own, attempting to extend the series to seven games. The Nets led throughout the game, toying with 8 to 10-point leads in the second half as the Spurs were desperately searching for a momentum swing to change their fate. They found one, thanks to Manu Ginobili. With slightly more than nine minutes remaining in the fourth quarter, the Spurs guard picked the Nets' Richard Jefferson clean at midcourt, resulting in a transition basket, cutting the Spurs deficit to six. Even though Rodney Rogers nailed a three-pointer to increase New Jersey's lead back to nine with 8:55 to play, a sense of revival among the Spurs players had already taken place. Robinson re-entered the game with 7:08 remaining and the 37-year-old who drew two charges on the defensive end in the third quarter, was determined to ensure that this would be his farewell performance. The Admiral grabbed seven rebounds in the remaining seven minutes as the Spurs overwhelmed the Nets. Stephen Jackson, the Spurs streaky shooting guard who was 0 for 3 on threes up to that point, finally found his touch, nailing three

three-pointers that helped propel the Spurs to their first lead of the night, 73-72 with 6:34 remaining in the game. It was a lead the Spurs would never relinquish. When the dust cleared, the Spurs had ran off an amazing 19-0 run.

"It all started on the defensive end with them," said Nets head coach Byron Scott, who saw his team go scoreless for a five-minute stretch during the Spurs run. "They got aggressive and we got out of our flow. We started rushing shots, started taking bad shots."

Duncan was a big reason why the Nets were out of sync on the offensive end. The Spurs' All-Star dominated the game in all phases, whether it was scoring, blocking shots,

controlling the boards or simply finding his teammates with pinpoint passing. Duncan finished two blocks shy of recording a quadruple-double, tallying 21 points, 20 rebounds, 10 assists and eight blocks. It was easily one of the greatest single-game performances in NBA Finals history

"IT'S ALMOST UNFAIR," SAID ROBINSON, WHO FINISHED WITH 13 POINTS AND 17 REBOUNDS. "WE ALWAYS EXPECT A GREAT, GREAT GAME FROM HIM AND HE JUST DELIVERS TIME AND TIME AGAIN."

Duncan also established an NBA Finals record with 32 blocks for the series, breaking the old mark of 30 set by Patrick Ewing of the New York Knicks who did it in seven games during the 1994 NBA Finals.

The Spurs received a big lift from point guard Speedy Claxton, who substituted for Tony Parker and scored 13 points and dished four assists in 23 minutes of play. Claxton was also on the court for the entire fourth quarter during the Spurs' comeback.

"Speedy must have made every shot he took," said Kidd. "He was big for them off the bench. He was a big X-factor for them throughout the series. If Tony [Parker] wasn't going they had Speedy to pick up the slack."

The championship celebration was particularly sweet for Kevin Willis, the Spurs 41-year-old backup forward who played 19 years, logging more than 1,300 games to reach his first ever NBA Finals.

"It was a long time coming," said Willis. "It was a loooooooong time coming. It's well worth the wait." 🏀

"MY LAST GAME, STREAMERS FLYING, WORLD CHAMPIONSHIP, HOW COULD YOU WRITE A BETTER SCRIPT THAN THIS? THIS IS UNBELIEVABLE."

DAVID ROBINSON

NEW JERSEY NETS

PLAYER	POS	MIN	FGM-A	3GM-A	FTM-A	REBOUNDS OFF	DEF	TOT	AST	PF	ST	TO	BS	PTS
JASON KIDD	G	42	8-20	3-9	2-2	2	2	4	7	4	1	0	0	21
KERRY KITTLES	G	34	5-12	2-6	4-4	0	4	4	2	2	3	0	0	16
RICHARD JEFFERSON	F	41	6-15	0-1	1-1	2	5	7	2	5	0	3	0	13
KENYON MARTIN	F	39	3-23	0-2	0-0	0	10	10	1	3	1	2	2	6
JASON COLLINS	C	25	2-5	0-0	0-0	0	3	3	0	4	1	1	1	4
Aaron Williams		16	2-4	0-0	0-0	1	0	1	2	4	1	1	1	4
Lucious Harris		15	0-1	0-1	2-4	1	1	2	0	1	0	1	0	2
Dikembe Mutombo		10	1-1	0-0	2-2	2	1	3	0	1	0	1	1	4
Rodney Rogers		8	1-2	1-1	0-0	0	0	0	0	1	0	0	0	3
Anthony Johnson		8	2-4	0-1	0-0	0	0	0	0	0	1	2	0	4
Tamar Slay		1	0-0	0-0	0-0	0	0	0	0	0	0	0	0	0
Brian Scalabrine		1	0-0	0-0	0-0	0	1	1	0	0	0	0	0	0
TOTAL		240	30-87	6-21	11-13	8	27	35	14	25	8	11	5	77
			(34.5)	(28.6)	(84.6)	Team Rebs: 11								

SAN ANTONIO SPURS

PLAYER	POS	MIN	FGM-A	3GM-A	FTM-A	REBOUNDS OFF	DEF	TOT	AST	PF	ST	TO	BS	PTS
STEPHEN JACKSON	G	35	7-13	3-7	0-0	0	3	3	0	3	1	6	0	17
TONY PARKER	G	24	2-6	0-0	0-0	0	2	2	2	0	0	3	0	4
TIM DUNCAN	F	46	9-19	0-1	3-5	4	16	20	10	2	0	4	8	21
BRUCE BOWEN	F	18	1-7	0-2	0-0	0	0	0	2	0	1	0	0	2
DAVID ROBINSON	C	31	6-8	0-0	1-4	4	13	17	1	2	0	1	2	13
Emanuel Ginobili		33	2-8	0-4	7-9	1	6	7	1	3	2	1	0	11
Speedy Claxton		23	5-8	0-0	3-4	0	1	1	4	2	0	2	1	13
Malik Rose		18	1-3	0-0	3-3	2	3	5	0	1	0	2	2	5
Steve Kerr		9	1-1	0-0	0-0	0	0	0	0	1	0	0	0	2
Danny Ferry		1	0-0	0-0	0-0	0	0	0	0	0	0	0	0	0
Steve Smith		1	0-1	0-1	0-0	0	0	0	0	0	0	0	0	0
Kevin Willis		1	0-0	0-0	0-0	0	0	0	0	0	0	0	0	0
TOTAL		240	34-74	3-15	17-25	11	44	55	20	14	4	19	13	88
			(45.9)	(20.0)	(68.0)	Team Rebs: 6								

ALL ACCESS

"This has been the ride of my life. There is no place to celebrate like San Antonio. I'm going to be up there in the stands with you all cheering them on next year."